Long live the Queen of Fre...
inspirational, Cherie's debt...
the dark pit of debt dragon...
freedom with "been-there, don't-do-that" wisdom.

CRAIG AND AMY GROESCHEL
Founders of LifeChurch.tv

In today's world, financial choices we thought would bring
happiness often turn into chains that keep us from experiencing
the freedom that is ours through Jesus. Cherie Lowe will give you
the practical tips, tools, and encouragement you need to break the
bondage of financial burdens and discover how to live a truly
abundant, joyful life.

HOLLEY GERTH
Bestselling author of *You're Going to Be Okay*

The tentacles of debt don't just burrow into pocketbooks and
bank accounts, they entangle our relationships, our attitudes, and
our hearts. This fresh look at living debt-free once and for all is
compelling, inspiring, and practical. You can't afford not to buy
this book.

MARGARET FEINBERG
Author of *Wonderstruck* and *Fight Back With Joy*

If you've ever had a panic attack trying to develop a budget, wanted to
get out of debt but don't know where to start, or said the words, "I'm
just not a numbers person," then you need to read this book today.
Cherie Lowe is a kind companion for a difficult journey. She helps
you make peace with your pocketbook as you learn to see the beauty
in a budget, and she does it with wisdom, grace, and a light heart.

EMILY P. FREEMAN
Author of *A Million Little Ways*

Cherie Lowe's incredible story of conquering her family's debt dragon is inspiring, entertaining, and filled with hope. Through practical tips and her own personal battle tales, you'll be reminded that financial freedom is indeed possible.

CLAIRE DIAZ-ORTIZ
Author and Silicon Valley innovator

A plethora of words come to mind after reading this incredible book: insightful, honest, practical, challenging, wise, and useful. Cherie Lowe tells her saga with humor, guts, and raw transparency. It is a story that will encourage you to face your own debt dragon with hope and determined courage.

KURT W. BUBNA
Pastor and author of *Epic Grace*

Slaying the Debt Dragon is an approachable guide to ridding your life of unnecessary debt. Not only are the debt-slaying strategies practical and doable, but the advice comes from a family who truly experienced the journey toward financial freedom. Cherie helps her readers set aside the guilt and shame of living in debt and gives a step-by-step guide to getting out of debt into financial freedom. There is no way that you cannot save money after reading this. For those struggling with debt, this book is filled with hope for a better life ahead. I can't recommend it highly enough!

AMY ALLEN CLARK
Author of *The Good Life for Less* and MomAdvice.com

Slaying the Debt Dragon is an honest, freeing, and entirely refreshing read. Cherie's story inspired me to reevaluate the way I view and spend money. Her wisdom is hard won, and is told with bold, witty authenticity.

MARY DeMUTH
Author of *The Wall Around Your Heart*

The humility and vulnerability revealed by Cherie in *Slaying the Debt Dragon* are refreshing and inviting. She has invited the world into her life by giving us a "look under the hood" of what it takes for the power of debt to lose its sting in our lives. By the end of this book, you'll be encouraged to press on to your own financial freedom because of her nonglamorous, authentically simple, and realistic journey that she has invited us to join.

RYAN JOHNSON
Lead Pastor of New City Church, Lawrenceville, Georgia

I read Cherie's story with my jaw dropped to the floor. The amount of debt she and her husband acquired is astounding, but the short amount of time in which they put their debt to death is astonishing and inspiring. Through her story and experience, Cherie will give *you* the practical steps you need to take to walk yourself right on up to the dragon and sling your sword into its mouth. She'll encourage you, give you hope, and hold your hand as you journey out of debt and into a life of financial freedom and wealth acquisition. Now, grab your sword and raise it with her . . . because she's about to teach you how to slay your debt dragon!

ERIN CHASE
Author of The $5 Dinner Mom Cookbook series

I've known Cherie and Brian Lowe since before they slayed their debt dragons. The freedom they enjoy now comes from employing the principles and advice that Cherie generously shares in this book. They're not just theories and platitudes but tried and true principles and habits that turned things around for the Lowes. The good news is that the information Cherie offers really works and can make all the difference in your financial future. Follow Cherie on this adventure—you won't regret it.

BRODIE TAPHORN
Associate pastor of Upper Arlington Lutheran Church, Columbus, Ohio

Cherie has given us two amazing gifts: motivation and direction! Throughout the book, you will hear Cherie's spunky voice proclaiming, "You can do it!" Many good resources tell you how to "eat the elephant" and even where to begin. But if knowing "how to" was enough, we would all be millionaires! In order to begin, we must believe the end of debt-free is truly possible. Out of the ashes of her family's own financial mistakes and despair, Cherie confidently says, "We did it, and you can too!" Prepare to be encouraged and empowered!

MICHAEL NAVE
Lead Pastor of Cornerstone Church, Marion, Illinois

With flair, candor, and humor, Cherie Lowe offers a field-tested plan to turn your finances around. Her real-life story, strategies, and no-nonsense advice will help you find the freedom you've been dreaming of.

SCOT LONGYEAR
Pastor of Maryland Community Church, Terre Haute, Indiana

SLAYING THE DEBT DRAGON

SLAYING
THE DEBT
DRAGON

How one family conquered their money monster
and found an inspired happily ever after

CHERIE LOWE

TYNDALE®
MOMENTUM

An Imprint of
Tyndale House Publishers, Inc.

Visit Tyndale online at www.tyndale.com.

Visit Tyndale Momentum online at www.tyndalemomentum.com.

Visit Cherie Lowe at www.queenoffree.net.

TYNDALE, Tyndale Momentum, and the Tyndale Momentum logo are registered trademarks of Tyndale House Publishers, Inc. Tyndale Momentum is an imprint of Tyndale House Publishers, Inc.

Slaying the Debt Dragon: How One Family Conquered Their Money Monster and Found an Inspired Happily Ever After

Published in association with the literary agency of The Fedd Agency, Inc., PO Box 341973, Austin, TX 78734.

Library of Congress Cataloging-in-Publication Data

Lowe, Cherie.
  Slaying the debt dragon : how one family conquered their money monster and found an inspired happily ever after / Cherie Lowe.
    pages cm
  Includes bibliographical references.
  ISBN 978-1-4143-9720-7 (paperback)
  1. Finance, Personal. 2. Consumer credit. 3. Debt. 4. Finance, Personal—Religious aspects—Christianity. I. Title.
  HG179.L5867 2014
  332.024´02—dc23   2014025165

Printed in the United States of America

20   19   18   17   16   15   14
7   6   5   4   3   2   1

To Brian, Anna, and Zoe.
You know the real me, and you love me anyway.
How great a gift I have been given in daily living the adventure of life
with you—from the mundane to the unreal. Let's always
have spontaneous dance parties in the kitchen and
value time together over any earthly thing.
Better than any amount in our bank account, better than the best
bargain I could ever find, you are a treasure beyond words.

Contents

Introduction *xiii*

Introduction

Fairy tales are more than true: not because they tell us that dragons exist, but because they tell us that dragons can be beaten.

PARAPHRASE OF A QUOTE BY G. K. CHESTERTON[1]

BEING IN DEBT is a lot like being in the dark.

I'm not talking about bedtime dark, where you can still see a stream of light from the moon or the gentle glow of a night-light in the hallway. No, being in debt is like sitting alone in darkness so pitch-black, so completely devoid of light, that you finally squeeze your eyes tightly shut, praying when you open them there will be some glow, even if it's just the faintest illumination.

Then there is the isolation. When you feel hopelessly in debt, lies like these creep into your head:

No one could have made *this* many mistakes.
No one else could feel *this* out of control.
No one could have been *that* dumb with their money.

No one else could have let a credit card balance spiral dizzily beyond reach (even though you were using it *only* for emergencies). No one else could have felt the pressure to keep up with others by spending money that was not her own. No one could feel this scared about not having a secure future. No one else could be under this kind of pressure.

So lonely. So in the dark.

You are *not* the only one struggling to escape the darkness of debt, even excessive debt. A great number of people have shared their lonely stories with me—either on my blog or in person—over the past five and a half years. A lot of them are slaying debt dragons right now or at least trying to figure out what weapons to use to begin the battle. And some have fought and won their battles already. There is actually a large community of people who make hard choices to get out of debt and spend less than they make every day.

But back to those feelings of darkness. When those "no one else could have" statements float around in your brain, you begin to believe the lie that you really are the only one who has this nasty debt problem. Then the gloom you're stumbling around in creeps into your very soul, along with its partners in crime, shame and guilt.

That darkness will keep you from sharing your story, preventing you from getting the help you need to get out of debt. It will also hinder you from offering hope to others who are on the same path, feeling just as alone as you do. Darkness is an evil fiend—a dragon, if you will—that casts some sort of spell paralyzing us all.

In the beginning, it was difficult for my husband, Brian, and me to "go public" with our story. I mean, come on—we haven't always been the people who have paid off $127,482.30 in debt. Back in April 2008, we were the people who *had* $127K+ of debt. It's much easier to share your story when you have kicked a few debt dragons in the teeth than when you have one (or twelve) breathing fire down your back.

And that's why I committed to continuing to tell our story, even after there was victory. Because I know what it's like to feel alone and in the dark.

You are not alone. Cast out the darkness and tell your story. Be honest with yourself and others about your finances so you can begin the path to victory over debt. Get the help and hope that you need to begin defeating your own debt dragons.

You see, the first step to getting out of debt doesn't involve elaborate spreadsheets. Honestly, it isn't about cutting up your credit cards, either. It's not even establishing an emergency fund. No, the first step is simply to lift your eyes up and believe that the *dragons can be beaten.*

If you'll allow me, I'd like to use the next few hours of your time to convince you that you can slay your debt dragon, no matter how ferocious, no matter how daunting in size and stature. Maybe you'll see a bit of yourself in our story. Maybe you'll discover that your attitudes about money have landed you in a dark financial dungeon. Maybe you'll realize that your spouse is not someone to battle against when it comes to finances, but instead your greatest ally and debt-slaying partner. Maybe this journey of gaining control of your money will actually bring the two of you closer together than you ever dreamed or imagined. And maybe you'll pick up a quick money-saving tip or two, which Brian and I either learned from our mistakes or gained during four long years of scaling back our lifestyle so we could pay off our huge debt.

Slaying the Debt Dragon isn't a quick fix. All worthwhile endeavors take time. It's not a complicated, smarty-pants economic treatise either. The steps I outline are practical and actually simple to follow if you dedicate yourself to the great quest of paying off those bills. Eliminating debt has less to do with the dollars in your pocket or the score on your IQ test than you realize. Stepping into financial freedom requires small, simple, gradual changes made

> Eliminating debt has less to do with the dollars in your pocket than with small, simple, gradual changes made over time and with resolve.

over time and with resolve. I hope you'll allow me to guide you on your journey by outlining the changes we made and showing how we stuck to those changes even when we felt challenged or overwhelmed.

For many years, our debt isolated us—from each other, from others with the same struggle, from God's best for our lives. Hook, line, and sinker, Brian and I bought the lie that we were alone. That lie prevented us from doing and being so many things. We lacked peace. We lacked unity. We lacked generosity. We lacked hope. I wish I could look you in the eyes and plead with you now to reject that lie. Don't choose isolation and entrapment. Don't choose the dark. Choose community and freedom. Through the words of this book, I pray you can begin the well-lit path to freedom.

Hans Christian Andersen said, "Every person's life is a fairy tale written by God's fingers." God wants to tell a story through my life. God wants to tell a story through your life. He even wants to tell it through your bank account. I want to invite you into my family's story, to hear our battle tales and to see the weapons we used to defeat our dragons. However, even more than that, I want you to step into your own story. Have hope that God can deliver you from debt and that He cares about every hair on your head and every penny in the bank. If He can keep the universe from spinning out of control, He can certainly handle the fact that you have amassed more financial obligations than you would care to admit on your Facebook status. He will provide for you if you take His hand and trust Him.

Our story is not your story. I have a feeling I will want to hear your story someday, because it is designed uniquely for who you are and the plan God has for *your* life.

Step into your story. Your financial happily ever after can begin today.

The light shines in the darkness, and the darkness has not overcome it.

JOHN 1:5, ESV

Chapter 1

ONCE UPON A TIME

Change is painful. Few people have the courage to seek out change. Most people won't change until the pain of where they are exceeds the pain of change.
DAVE RAMSEY, *The Total Money Makeover*

ONCE UPON A TIME . . . every great story has one. No matter the "happily ever after" or the many details in between, it simply wouldn't be a great tale without a "once upon a time." This is my family's once upon a time. Honestly, though, our story is fairly ordinary rather than fairy-tale extraordinary. However, I often need to answer the "How in the world did you end up with $127,000 in debt?" question before I dive into the methods we used to eliminate it. So without further ado:

Once upon a time . . .

Fresh out of college and married for only a month, Brian and I moved to a new city so he could begin law school. We were both unemployed and incredibly clueless about finances. We were living on love and chips and salsa from Chi-Chi's, which was the restaurant nearest to our less-than-luxury apartment. I landed a job working full-time for a church while Brian went to school, clerking whenever his schedule allowed. For the next three years, most days seemed to follow that same pattern: Work. Chi-Chi's. School. Repeat. We didn't live recklessly. We didn't buy a million-dollar home. We didn't wear designer clothes. Due to the hectic nature of higher education and church ministry (okay, we were also lazy, and I really liked seafood enchiladas), we had a serious dining-out problem, but overall we weren't wild with our resources.

Our main plan for our finances, though, was not having a plan. Chalk it up to newlywed ignorance or a lack of financial literacy or that we were still living more like children than adults. But that lack of a plan was our first big mistake, and after a while it caught up with us. The brakes would go out on the car. *Pull out the Visa!* When we didn't have enough cash to go out with friends for dinner? *Well, hello there, my little plastic compadre.* Doctor's visit? *Guess we should charge it. I mean, we have to go, right?*

Eventually, Brian finished law school and found a good job. A couple of months later, I gave birth to Anna, our amazing first daughter who turned our hearts inside out. I quit my job to stay home with her, so we never even got the chance to fall into "the two-income trap."[1] We bought a house. In the eyes of the world, we were living the American dream. Graduated from college? Check. Married? Check. Law school, baby, home owners? Check, check, and check. These were all things that we were supposed to do as young adults. We were nailing this grown-up thing.

Then the student loans came due. We deferred them.

They came due again.

It seems a bit astonishing to me now that we continued to live without any real financial planning for the next five years. We celebrated birthdays and anniversaries. We wished each other Merry Christmas. I went to graduate school, and when Anna was a toddler, I took on a part-time job at a different church. We went on vacations.

We bought a new car. Life moved along as it often does, in the day-to-day of grocery shopping and laundry, holidays, and weekends.

Don't get me wrong. Brian and I weren't living in a stress-free, la-di-da world. While we loved each other and even enjoyed our lives as a small family, there was this underlying tension that I can't quite describe. There were no big blowup fights about money. But there was an occasional angst-filled, passive-aggressive moment or two along the way. *Did we really need that? You bought what?* Brian and I rarely discussed how much was in the bank, let alone any goals for our finances.

Enter the part of me that wishes I could sensationalize our story for you. I once was asked if I had bought something I loved in every color and maxed out our credit cards on designer shoes. That's simply not me. I wish I could tell you that we went on some killer vacation with beautiful ocean vistas and a pricey, high-flying skydiving experience. Didn't happen. Did we buy a yacht? Nope. How about an RV? Nope. Did we take our kids to Disney World every week? month? year? Nope, nope, and nope. Did we have awesome computers and smartphones and amazing technology in our home? Uh-uh. Was our house a McMansion? *Pbfft.*

Aside from the mortgage on our home—a small and very modest 1950s brick ranch—our debt consisted of what most people would consider run-of-the-mill expenses. Oddly enough, approximately ten months before we launched into our debt-slaying journey, I was contemplating returning to work full-time. In my mind, employment would help us "get ahead" financially, and Anna was ready to begin kindergarten anyway. We could relieve some of the pressure we were feeling and maybe be able to afford a few of the extras so many friends seemed to regularly enjoy. Then unexpectedly I discovered I was pregnant, and everything changed. God had blessed us with new life.

He'd also given us another reason to think seriously about how to dig ourselves out of debt, which was comprised primarily of four large obligations. We owed close to $89,000 in combined student loans, including my husband's undergrad and graduate school debt as well as a loan from one semester of my collegiate experience. (Thanks, Mom and Dad, for covering the other seven semesters!)

Then we owed over $16,500 on one major credit card. Again, I wish we had something to show for it. But there's no killer house addition, no walk-in closet filled with stylish clothes, no four-wheelers or vacation photos. We simply nickeled-and-dimed our way into five figures of debt—spent to cover household repairs, groceries, small gifts, dining out, new brakes and tires for the car, all very *boring* stuff.

We also had a car loan to the tune of about $12,000. Our vehicle was quite modest by our reckless standards, so we'll call that one a grace-filled "oops."

The final piece was the medical debt. In mid-March 2008, our second daughter, Zoe, made her arrival. She brought life, grace, and energy into our lives. She also brought a big heap of medical bills amounting to $5,700. We hadn't planned on that either.

On top of these four major obligations were a few minor debts like a $2,200 root canal for me (that was no fun *and* expensive), $1,000 in furniture we had purchased on a payment plan, $100 on a department store card, and interest paid along the way.

While not so glamorous, these debts totaled well over $127,000, a figure that typically makes people's eyes bulge bigger than Homer Simpson's when I share it with them.

I nearly passed out myself when Brian first showed me the bottom-line debt total. It wasn't during a serious moment at the kitchen table or even during a budget meeting in our living room, where eventually we would bury our noses in a laptop, crunching numbers and trying to figure out what we could cut from our already simple lifestyle. Instead we were standing inches from each other in our bedroom. In many ways, though, our hearts were miles apart at that moment. Motivated by the pressure of one more mouth to feed and one more child to put through college someday, Brian had begun some serious number crunching. Poised next to his dresser, he stared down at a white legal pad. On it was scratched out how much we owed and to whom. The list seemed very long and the numbers very large.

Inside, I was trying not to completely freak out. I'm not of much use in high-stress situations. I actually ran around in circles once after accidentally setting something on fire in our oven. Seriously, I waved my hands in the air like a lunatic and repeated, "What are we going to do?! What are we going to do?!" while Brian calmly put out the fire with baking soda. He handles crisis moments with much more grace than I do.

While the ball of panic built up in my gut, I resisted the urge to repeat my "the oven's on fire!" theatrics. I realized I hadn't ever thought about our debt in its totality. I was merely functioning month to month, making sure the bills were paid and there were groceries in the refrigerator. Sure, I occasionally did a little "creative" financing, paying a bill just a bit late so we could make ends meet until the next pay period, but I was simply clueless as to the size of our debt.

While seeing that enormous total on Brian's legal pad was my wake-up call, he had first begun strategizing our debt-slaying journey two years prior. His moment of clarity came as we were sitting in a large-chain bookstore on a low-key date. While browsing, Brian pulled the book *The Total Money Makeover* by Dave Ramsey from a shelf and walked it back to the overstuffed chairs where we had been sitting. I can't remember what I was reading that night, though I'm sure it was—*ahem*—significant at the time.

Brian read the entire Dave Ramsey book.[2] He put it back on the shelf. Our date ended. As we headed back to our car, I had no idea that my husband was already considering battle plans.

He soon became an avid fan of Dave Ramsey's radio show.

Inspired by what he was learning, Brian began to cast the vision for us to pay off all of our debt. He asked me to read the book. He encouraged me to listen to podcasts. To help us dream big, he began posing questions like "What could we do with all the money we'd save if we weren't paying so much interest each month?" He never demanded. He never dictated. He was patient and kind. He never forced me to do anything.

Brian can talk a good game. He asks questions for a living. His words and thoughts were definitely compelling. However, what spoke volumes to me was the way he began to change his own personal habits with money. Again, he did this without coercing or even convincing me to do the same. I began to sit up and take notice.

In early 2008, Brian stopped using the one major credit card we had. I tried to use it only for reimbursable work expenses. Unfortunately, I rarely made a payment from the check I was given for those expenses. Not only that, but I felt like a heel for using my credit card when my spouse had stopped using his—even though he didn't say anything. (Keep that in mind if you are praying for new financial direction in your marriage. Change begins with you. Not your spouse or anyone else.) So in February, I used the card for the very last time.

At some point in March, we jointly made the decision to get serious about beginning what we would eventually call our "debt-slaying journey." It appeared to be a less-than-optimal time to begin such an undertaking. Our younger daughter was due to make her appearance any day. Babies are so adorable, but they are ridiculously pricey. Medical bills, diapers, gadgets and gizmos you never knew you needed, as well as drive-through dinners on the nights you're too exhausted to cook—the expenses are limitless and typically unexpected.

It was probably the worst time to begin paying off debt. But honestly, is there ever a good time to start? There will always be an unexpected illness or a car that explodes, a birth, a death, a washing machine that goes bonkers. *There is no good time to begin paying off debt. There is only today.*

I am thankful our situation hadn't spiraled out of control to the point where we lost our house or our car. Looking back now, I know that both were very real pos-

There is no good time to begin paying off debt. There is only today.

sibilities. Had Brian lost his job, had illness struck our family, or had we encountered a significant repair or tragedy, we could easily have folded, broken, and shattered—financially, emotionally, and spiritually. Fortunately, our internal unease prompted some serious self-examination before we hit a crisis point.

Even so, our situation was sobering. By Brian's best estimates, it would take us fifteen years to pay off all of our debt; nine if we really hustled. He adjusted his withholdings at work, which freed up an extra $100 per month. That meant we would no longer receive a refund, but we wouldn't have to pay anything extra at tax time either. It wasn't a whole lot compared to what we owed, but it was money we weren't using to live. On April 2, 2008, away we went, beginning by tackling our smallest debt first.[3]

I rarely vocalized them then, but I had multiple fears in the early days. As I stared at the columns of figures Brian had scribbled on his legal pad, a number of terrifying thoughts tumbled through my troubled soul: *How did we end up in this mess? What if we never pay all this off? What will we do if another major unexpected expense comes up? Will we ever have fun again?* (I know, the last one is a very noble fear, right?)

Then again, continuing on our current path didn't seem much better: What could happen to our family if we kept the same spending patterns, persisting in our non-plan plan?

While it might seem wishy-washy and semipathetic, before we

began the process of getting out from under debt, I had to face those fears and ask for forgiveness. I'm not talking about debt forgiveness in the financial sense, but in the emotional and spiritual sense. After pondering all the self-condemning and "what if?" questions, feelings of guilt, remorse, and insecurity gushed into my heart and brain. *How could I have been so stupid? How could I have made so many unwise choices with money? Why was I so selfish in needing one more thing?*

Don't get me wrong—remorse is a good thing. It made me uncomfortable enough to realize, *What we're doing now isn't working. Why not tackle paying off all our debt?* However, if guilt paralyzes you, it is unproductive. So at some point, I had to shake it off and rub some dirt in it (or at least that's what the coach and my dad always advised), to move on to the next step.

For me, this was a two-step process of (1) admitting to myself, *Yes, I was wrong*, and (2) realizing that we had to begin where we were right then. To get out of debt, Brian and I needed to change our behaviors that stemmed from our poor judgment, trusting God to provide avenues for us to follow to clean up our financial blunders.

Presenting the Queen of Free

As you can see, our "once upon a time" story didn't have a dramatic beginning. Brian and I didn't have a colossal fight followed by a tearful time of prayer, where we resolved to follow God's plan for our money. That's a great story, but it simply isn't ours. Instead, we began by taking small steps of obedience—changing our behaviors, seeking forgiveness, and acknowledging our overwhelming desire for hope for our financial future.

One of my first small steps included reducing our spending, especially in the area of groceries and household goods. I set out to learn how to use coupons and, *even better*, to score anything and everything I could for free.

I've always loved anything free. Who doesn't? When I was a young girl, I purchased an amazing paperback at my elementary school's book fair. To me, its pages contained the secrets of the universe. Eight-year-old Cherie squealed with glee when she learned that there were actually companies who would send you items absolutely free if you wrote a letter and included a SASE (that's "self-addressed stamped envelope" for you young whippersnappers).

The advent of the Internet brought my quest for free to a whole new level of excitement—particularly once we took on our debt. I began sharing my freebie finds with friends and family via e-mail. More and more people began requesting to be added to my already lengthy list of names. Inadvertently, I left someone out from time to time. After one too many "I wish I had known about that" messages, many punctuated with sad-faced emoticons, I decided to begin sharing my love of all things free on a personal blog.

After reading one of my tips on Facebook (if my memory serves me correctly, it was a free roast beef sandwich at Arby's), a friend told me how much he appreciated my daily tips. "You're like the Queen of Free!" he remarked. I liked it. It was a little girly but still powerful. The title stuck, and in August of 2008, I launched *Queen of Free*. In the early days, the site was completely anonymous, a place where a cartoon version of me shared one freebie a day. By the end of the year, I was offering other ideas for frugal living, as well as sharing bits and pieces of our story. Since I was now the Queen of Free, naturally Brian became the King of Free and my daughters the Princess Eldest and the Princess Youngest.[4] And debt, our gargantuan nemesis? We started calling that the dragon. (But we'll get to that later.)

Through the world of blogging, I began to discover that my family and I were not fighting alone. The myth of isolation began to fall away when I recognized we were standing with dozens and then hundreds and then thousands of allies—women and men who wanted to wage war on debt too. Each time we paid off a debt, they cheered great hurrahs of victory. When we stumbled and fell, they whispered, "Me, too." I was surprised to learn that the community of co-battlers included people I actually knew but who had also been fearful of sharing their stories. Others I have yet to meet face-to-face, but my heart powerfully links to their journeys.

After my site had been up and running for a number of months, a sweet friend from the blogging community was shocked to learn I didn't have an actual crown. She brought me a plastic tiara to a conference we were both attending, and I've worn it proudly many times over the past five years (even on the news once or twice). I know it seems silly, but every time I wear that crown, it gives me strength. It speaks volumes about where we have been and where we are headed. Yet I don the little plastic tiara knowing that, had God not intervened, our fairy tale would have ended as a horror story. I am confident that God placed us in a "for such a time as this"[5] moment so we could share our experience with you.

Turning the Page to Begin a New Story

Perhaps you're at the very beginning of your own debt-slaying journey. I know how challenging it is to admit to anyone that you have made a mess of your life. And sometimes it's even difficult to confess to a loving Creator that you have wrecked your finances. You can't give like you want to give because you simply are stretched too thin. You don't have the peace that the Bible describes because you're overwhelmed with all of the "what ifs" of life. I know. I've been there.

If that's where you are today, you must say you're sorry to whomever your debt has affected—God, your spouse, yourself, your parents. Then embrace their forgiveness and turn the page to begin a new story, resolving to change both your mind and your behavior when it comes to money. You will feel stronger and be better prepared to wage your battle against debt. Remember that this type of forgiveness isn't just about apologizing and receiving grace. It's also about daily being willing to change what you do and maybe even rejecting lifelong practices and philosophies.

Once you total up how much you owe, you may be completely overwhelmed. You may even feel paralyzed when you see an exact figure on paper. That very fear begs you to quit before you begin. It yearns for you to see the number and run and hide. Odds are, even if you don't owe over $100K like we did, you're probably not happy or even comfortable with the grand total.

When you feel as if you owe your very soul and are imprisoned by debt, you sense danger all around you. One false move and your house of cards will fall apart. One gentle breeze and the illusion you've built for yourself—*We're just like everyone else. We're doing okay. It's not that bad*—will knock you off your feet.

But remember, there is no good time to begin paying off debt. There is only today. There will always be an upcoming expense, a needed replacement, a current life struggle. If you convince yourself that there's an ideal moment waiting for you to begin your personal debt-slaying journey, you'll never pay down a dime. Instead, you will continue to be as broke as a joke. At some point, you *must* begin your own "once upon a time." If you never turn that page to begin your own adventure, you'll never find your happily ever after.

Debt-Slaying Strategies

✓ Set aside a half hour to sit down with your spouse (if you're married) or a trusted friend (if you're not) and discuss:

- Your current financial strategy. Is not having a plan your plan?

- What first step you (not your spouse) could take to begin bringing your finances under control or to improve your current practices. Make sure the change is small, gradual, concrete, and sustainable.

✓ Find a legal pad or blank sheet of paper. Or if you're more comfortable with technology, open a spreadsheet, budgeting software, or an app. List every debt you have. Be brave. Be bold. Don't let fear control your future.

Chapter 2

DEBT-DEFYING DUOS

Friendship is a deep oneness that develops when two people, speaking the
truth in love to one another, journey together to the same horizon.
TIMOTHY KELLER, *The Meaning of Marriage*

LONG AGO AND FAR AWAY, when I wasn't a queen but a mere maiden, Brian
did something so subtle, so simple that neither of us could have
imagined its significance. In fact, he barely remembers the occurrence today.

We were on our second date. As we entered the auditorium at
the movie theater, Brian gently put his hand on the small of my back
and led me to our seats. Truth be told, Brian hadn't initiated any
physical contact before then, not even elementary-school-style hand-
holding. Yet his touch felt as natural as if he had done it a thousand
times before. Funny, lightly touching my back doesn't seem like such
a big deal, but it sent both chills down my spine and a message to my
brain that this young man was different. You see, he was leading me.

He wasn't guiding me with a push. His touch was gentle, and I
could have easily broken away if I'd so desired. Brian didn't force me

into a seat. He didn't say, "Sit down, woman, and like it!" Nope, he just gently and quietly led me to our destination.

Flash forward seven or eight years. Once again, he was the one who quietly led us into our debt-slaying journey. He didn't bark orders or push me into something I didn't understand. He led with a gentle hand to the small of my back, asking nonthreatening questions like

Would you read this book?
Could we talk about our finances?
What would we do if we didn't have to worry about payments?
How could having extra money to give change our world and
  the world around us?

Steadily and surely, he led our family out of the darkness and into the light. He led with humility and hard work. He led with an amazing example and kind words. He led with the willingness to listen and receive feedback. He led with creativity and an eye toward where we excelled and where we could improve. All the while, his hand was there, reassuring me that we would be okay, that this path led to freedom, and that the joy tomorrow would be worth the sacrifice today.

Now don't misunderstand me: To slay the debt dragon, you do *not* need to be married. You are certainly capable of paying off all of your debt, with or without a spouse. But if you are married, you both need to be behind this effort from the get-go. You must be committed to work together to pay off your debt. Otherwise, even if you are successful in such a mammoth task without the support and participation of your spouse, more than likely your marriage will be over soon after you slay the debt dragon. If you and your spouse don't yet agree on the necessity of paying off your debt, don't despair. Committing yourselves equally to this endeavor is a process—and one that probably neither of you saw coming on your wedding day.

I don't know any couple who began their life together dreaming about ways they could fall into or dig themselves out of debt. When I walked down the aisle, all donned in lacy white, such thoughts were far from my heart. I could see only stars and rainbows, puffy hearts and the letters *M-r-s* in front of my new name.

Looking back, it's clear that the key Scripture reading at our wedding was downright prophetic, though I didn't see it at the time:

> Two are better than one, because they have a good return
> for their labor: If either of them falls down, one can help
> the other up. But pity anyone who falls and has no one to
> help them up. Also, if two lie down together, they will keep
> warm. But how can one keep warm alone? Though one may
> be overpowered, two can defend themselves. A cord of three
> strands is not quickly broken. (Ecclesiastes 4:9-12, NIV)

I had long loved this passage for its beauty and turn of phrase, for the symbolic image of the binding of two souls with God in a three-strand cord. When those words were read as Brian and I stood at the front of the sanctuary, the idea of the two of us becoming one sounded enchanting—something straight out of a fairy tale.

You know what happened, right? A week, a month, a year, nearly a decade into our relationship, those old notions of romance were overrun with dirty underwear on the bathroom floor and all our mundane household tasks. We needed more than rainbows and stars to hold our marriage and our faith together. If we were going to pay off debt successfully, we needed more than puffy hearts, too. Brian and I had to unite, ready to help each other do what was necessary to get our finances under control. And we had to look to the third strand—God Himself—to keep us knitted together on the days when we disagreed or were discouraged.

How did we get there? You may recall from chapter 1 that Brian was ready to take on the challenge of getting out of debt before I was. That may seem like an odd reality for the Queen of Free to admit. Yet it's true. But before you think me to be a complete grouch and naysayer, consider this: I wasn't antagonistic about it. And I certainly wasn't happy about having so much debt. No one says, "When I grow up, I want to have over $100,000 in debt!" or "I'm overjoyed to have such a heavy financial burden hanging from my neck. It's swell!" At the same time, I couldn't wrap my head around exactly how we would ever pay it off. After all, I picked up the groceries, bought the girls' clothes, and paid the bills. I knew we were barely making ends meet. There seemed to be so very little wiggle room in our current situation—and the last time I checked, $127K was a whole lot of coin. Where was all of that money going to come from?

In fact, Brian had to wait two long years after first reading *The Total Money Makeover* before I was ready to commit to kicking debt in the teeth with him. I know he must have been frustrated at times. If you're in the same position—alarmed by your debt and poised to wage war against it while your spouse resists—I sympathize. If you have a gung ho spouse who's ready to dive in and yet you're dragging your feet—I understand. Waging war against debt is oh-so-discouraging when the vision for finances in your marriage is not the same for both spouses.

If you're the one who is so excited about the potential of slaying your own debt dragon that you've already outlined fifteen steps your family can take to begin this journey, I have one piece of advice: *slow down*. Remember when your parents forced you to clean your room as a little kid? Remember how long it took you? How you hated every single second that passed on the clock because you wanted to be outside running through the sprinkler, not picking up your toys? Forced debt-slaying journeys are no different. Sure, the job might get done in the long run, but no one will have any fun, and you might end up in the exact same place once again, both reluctantly cleaning up a mess.

Interestingly, getting your husband or wife on board to pay off debt may have more to do with what you *don't do* than what you do. Here's what I know *won't* work:

Nagging. Ever build a vinegar-and-baking-soda volcano for the science fair? If baking soda is your current financial situation, then vinegar is your nagging. You might get a result, but more than likely it will be

> Getting your husband or wife on board to pay off debt may have more to do with what you *don't do* than what you do.

an unpredictable explosion that will make a big mess all over the floor. No one ever did anything willingly due to a nag. Nagging builds up resentment in a relationship. It kills intimacy. It leads nowhere good, very quickly. Quit it. Now.

Disregarding your spouse's knowledge. If you have no idea how much milk costs per gallon, you shouldn't set the grocery budget. If you have never purchased shoes for your child, you shouldn't decide what should be spent on a pair of new kicks. If you have never looked at the electric bill during the month of July when the air conditioner runs nonstop, you shouldn't have an opinion on how much is "about right" to budget for utilities.

Does this mean that you check out and have no voice in the budgeting process at all? Absolutely not. What it does mean is that both spouses should be active participants in decision making. The managing of joint household finances is pursued one day at a time, one expense at a time. Your spouse may not know how much it really costs to run your household. Don't angrily give him or her the "what for." Instead, share receipts, shop together, and look at bank statements together. Also, realize that there's always room for improvement, even in your personal finance practices. You might need to see where milk is the most inexpensive this week. Is there a coupon for those shoes? Do they *really* need to be name brand? Is your air conditioner clean so it runs efficiently? In a spirit of kindness and with the aim of unity, ask if you don't understand an expense; likewise, explain an expense that your spouse doesn't understand.

> The managing of joint household finances is pursued one day at a time, one expense at a time.

Bringing up Kool-Aid stuff. I'm not sure when this phrase originated in our household, but we deemed "Kool-Aid stuff" the act of rehashing "we thought they were already resolved" issues—especially those surrounding money—during a fight. Those disagreements happened so long ago, it was like we were little kids drinking Kool-Aid, sitting on the steps. We learned to *let the problem or conflict at hand stand alone.* With everything that is within you, resist the urge to bring up problems of the past. You know you are treading in Kool-Aid waters when you hear words like "You said you wouldn't _____ again." Or "This is just like last time when you _____." Whenever you sit down to discuss finances, focus only on the present situation.

Forcing change. Often when we so passionately have a vision for our future, we begin to press hard in an attempt to manipulate others into doing what we want them to do. Strong-arming change might yield a short-term effect that pleases you, but it will never lead to long-term harmony.

Let's just say, for instance, that "someone" wants everyone in her household to be more intentional about taking their laundry to the laundry room. Said individual (who may or may not have red hair) could angrily huff and puff about how no one ever does anything to help around this place, with her harsh words leading everyone to fear her footfall. Her family quickly picks up their unmentionables and soggy towels just to get her to close her mouth. There is short-term relief through a forced change. However, the overall vision of why laundry must be placed in the proper receptacles is not delivered. Tomorrow, the same pattern recurs. Dirty laundry. Angry redhead. Fearful children. Baskets filled. Until the passion for an effective laundry system is shared by all, there will be only insanity and no harmony in ~~our~~ this random red-haired woman's home.

Going radio silent. When we really want to exact revenge on someone, many of us will shut down and say nothing at all. Of course, that always causes us more harm than the people we intend to injure. One of Brian's favorite quips is "The death of communication is the birth of resentment."[1] Don't use silence as a weapon; if you do, you will begin to resent each other. In fact, you must attempt to overcommunicate with your spouse while paying off debt. Keep a tone of love in your words and monitor them carefully.

Maybe you've avoided every single one of my "what not to do" traps. Maybe every word that trickles from your mouth is seasoned with love. Maybe you're so kind and loving to your spouse, even though he or she remains resistant to change, that your neighbors have built a shrine to your sainthood. Or maybe not.

> **"The death of communication is the birth of resentment."**

It may sound like a cliché or a spiritual Band-Aid, but if your spouse is resistant or even downright hostile when it comes to finances in your marriage, have you considered praying? I know firsthand that God is bigger than money. His power to change hearts reaches far beyond our meager efforts. Wouldn't you rather see God, not you, change your husband's or wife's heart and mind about debt?

If your spouse isn't yet on board, get on your knees—not to beg your spouse to follow your plan but to ask God to draw him or her to His best plan for your lives and to give him or her a vision that extends far beyond your checkbook or savings account. One of the prayers in our marriage has always been, *God, please bring the changes You want in my spouse. If You don't change my spouse, then change me.*

From Frugality to Freedom

I want to pause for just a moment and chat with those of you who might still be a little resistant to the idea of taking on the debt dragon. Maybe you feel frightened. After all, changing the way you spend money (or don't spend money) is scary. Perhaps you feel your spouse values money more than he or she values you. Or it could be that you are much like I was—you simply don't see how it's possible. Deep down you may fear the perceived scarcity that such a major life overhaul will bring. These are all valid fears. I've been there and done that with worry as deep as the ocean, times fourteen.

At times during our journey, I felt like frugality equaled scarcity. (Ever notice how similar sounding the words *scarcity* and *scary* are?)

Frugal—the very word can make us shudder. Believing we lack essentials or will miss out on something is terrifying. The fear of scarcity empties shelves before snowstorms and causes fistfights on Black Friday. We buy into the lie that someone else will purchase our something special and we will be left sad and lonely. *Operating from a mind-set of scarcity will create an enormous vacuum in our souls.* To fill that void, we begin to reach for anything or anyone to stuff inside the empty space. Wildly, we scrape and scratch at people, things, hobbies, or addictions—anything to take the edge off the fear that we'll be left with nothing.

When beginning to learn how to live with less, fearing frugality is pretty common. So it might surprise you to discover that the word *frugal* originates from the Latin word *frui*, which means "to enjoy,

DEBT-SLAYING DUO

RYAN AND AMBER, 37 AND 36
PARENTS OF DANIEL, 8; NATALIE, 6;
ALLISON, 3

PAID OFF $161,000

A career military family, Ryan and Amber have already faced adversity most couples will never know. Early in their marriage Ryan was deployed to both Kuwait and Iraq. Even now, Amber, a homeschooling mom, sometimes needs to fill both parenting roles while Ryan trains for military engagements. With all this family juggles, it would have been easy for them to ignore the debt they had racked up. Instead, facing it head on, they paid off $161,000 in fifty-seven months.

Why slay the debt dragon?

Even though they felt like they had "great" interest rates, Ryan and Amber spent well over $1,000 of their house-hold income per month on interest alone. Their financial choices were extremely restricted because of their heavy debt load. Ryan and Amber began to dream big dreams together, thinking about what they could spend *that* money on, if it wasn't being forked over to make payments.

What kept them going?

One of the biggest joys of Ryan and Amber's debt-slaying journey came from being able to share their success and help others. Their excitement spilled over as they told their story to church and military family support groups. Since their journey was rather long, Ryan and Amber occasion-ally took short breaks from penny-pinching to go on camping trips. They paid for these getaways with cash. These small milestone celebrations fueled their appetite for complete freedom, pushing them on toward their goal.

What was most challenging?

No matter how you slice it, paying off $161,000 isn't an easy task. Ryan admits that battling debt over such a long period required focus that was often difficult to maintain. So many times it felt as if their efforts made no difference and success seemed out of reach. Amber often struggled to find free or low-cost activities for the family's three young children.

How did they celebrate?

After paying off their final debt, Ryan and Amber saved up enough money in just a few months to take a cruise. This fabulous vacation allowed them to celebrate the conclusion of their debt-slaying journey, together with their three children and extended family. Those big dreams of "what else we could do" finally started coming true for this family.

Their encouragement and advice for you

Amber says, "Start small and build. Do *not* try to do everything all at once. Don't try to do extreme couponing. Ease yourself into the process and just get what you *need*. Start planning your meals based on what is on sale at the grocery store and see how much money you can save." Ryan recommends sticking with the plan, no matter how discouraged you become or even if you make a misstep. He says, "If you fall off the wagon or backslide a little, take a breath and then keep on going. If you want to commit to a complete transformation of your finances and change your life, then you are in it for the long haul. For us, this was an entire change in attitude. Our debt load was more than our mortgage. Now that we have tasted that victory, we know there's nothing we can't do!"

How has paying off debt changed their marriage?

I was overwhelmed by Amber's honest words of encouragement: "For me, paying it off together meant that we were *really* one in our marriage." Ryan admits that prior to beginning this journey of commitment, he didn't truly know what it took to run their household. Once they were armed with a common purpose and understanding of the budget, Ryan gained confidence that he and Amber were on the right path—together. "That trust allowed me to focus more energy at work and excel." Now that they're out of debt, Amber says, "I don't have to worry about Ryan getting mad about money or arguing about the budget. I don't feel like it's *his* money since he's the primary bread-winner. We are truly together." Their financial unity recently allowed them to move into a bigger house, something they never would have been able to do with their finances out of control.

profit by, delight in." It's the same root from which we draw words like *fruit, fructose*, and *fruition*. Living simply is sweet for your soul. It's a pursuit you can delight in *and* enjoy.

There were *so* many times in our debt-slaying journey when my eyes shifted toward our lack instead of our abundance. Signing on to Facebook, I'd see friends on vacation or at the movies or at a new restaurant.

> Living simply is sweet for your soul. It's a pursuit you can delight in *and* enjoy.

It was easy to enviously imagine myself in their shoes or throw myself a grand pity party because my family couldn't afford to do the same. I had to learn to fight that urge—to realize that I was bound for more than temporary fun or trendy pleasures.

The best thing I learned to do when scarcity filled my soul with fear was to reach toward Jesus. *He came to proclaim the Good News that we will never be left alone, sad, and with nothing.* Certainly, even when you have a relationship with Christ, you will still encounter fear at times. But can I be straightforward with you about the fear of scarcity that tends to develop once you wage war against debt? The truth is, if you are successfully going to pay off debt, you *will* go "without" from time to time.

But let's be honest, friends: Going without dining at a restaurant is not the same as going without food. Going without a vacation is not the same thing as going without a bed to sleep in at night. On a morning when the high temperature is predicted to be -11°F, I'm very much reminded that going without a cute new coat is not the same thing as going without heat in my home. In fact, going without something while you pay off debt just might be the key for drawing you closer to the Creator of the universe, knowing that you and your family will be not only okay, but well cared for and even lavished with great love. It's really all about how you look at whatever you already have. Put off the old eyes of looking at the world with that scarcity lens and put on your new frugal eyes, realizing there is plenty to enjoy within your home and even to share with others.

You or your spouse may not overcome your fear of scarcity overnight; however, recognizing and discussing it could bring you closer together. Whether you are united in your desire to overcome your debt or still at odds about what that means, invite God into your battle. When you do, you will be able to tap into His power and strength—though not in the way I expected when we started our fight.

In the early days, I begged and pleaded with God to make our debt go away. Surely He could send us a miracle check or a mysterious windfall. It never happened. Did that mean God didn't answer my prayers? Highly unlikely.

God used both prayer and the experience of paying off debt not just to change our finances, but to change my heart. Unfortunately, it didn't happen quickly. Turns out, I'm a pretty tough nut to crack. Contentment can still evade me. Greed and envy find a playground in my soul more often than I'd care to admit. Sometimes my thoughtlessness can result in not saving as much as I could. I'm far from where I should be, but I'm not where I once was either.

Taking On the Dragon

Willingness to lead (not shove) and to be led (not pulled along) are crucial mind-sets for married couples who are working to get out of debt. At times, each of you will exhibit strengths neither of you knew you had. Sometimes, one person will lead while the other one steps back, tired from the daily struggle. The next day, your roles may be reversed. What's essential is that neither of you push or push back, but rather that you work together.

And it's not all hard work either. Yes, personal finance is filled with cold, hard facts—columns, balances, and numbers all must be a part of your debt-slaying journey—but it also presents the opportunity for couples to dream together.

By now you know that one of the best things Brian did was to encourage me to imagine what our lives could be like without debt. What would it be like if we didn't have that car payment? What if our student loans weren't hanging around our necks like a heavy, rusty chain? What change might we bring to our family or our world if we weren't stretched so thin? Dreams motivate us. They give us a piece of the future to hold on to when the present seems too frightening.

> Dreams motivate us. They give us a piece of the future to hold on to when the present seems too frightening.

In fact, visualizing your future may be just as vital as aggressively crunching numbers. Brian and I also found it immensely motivating to visualize our present. Here's what that looked like for us. To this day, we keep two insanely important pieces of family history magneted to the side of our refrigerator. Intentionally placed, we can see

SIX WAYS TO KEEP YOUR MARRIAGE HEALTHY WHILE PAYING OFF DEBT

1. **Put the kids to bed on time each night.** You might not have a big date-night budget, but you can still have intentional time with your spouse on a regular basis. Now, more than ever, you will need it. It takes some extra effort, but establish a family time clock that includes prompt and regular routines to safeguard that evening time.

2. **Move together.** Exercise was a big part of our debt-slaying journey. Move on a regular basis, either together or individually. Schedule time for it, encourage your spouse to find regular physical activity that he or she loves, and make it easier for each other with no guilt trips and leading by example. Your minds, bodies, and hearts will thank you for it. The connection between paying off debt and exercising may seem fuzzy at first, but taking care of your body brings many benefits:

   • You'll be sick less often and have fewer chronic health problems. Less sickness = fewer doctors' visits, tests, and prescriptions, and more income.

   • You'll fill some of your time. Rather than battling the desires that come from scanning social media or watching TV, you'll keep moving and gain extra energy. Face it, to pay off debt you need to work harder than you ever have. Exercise refreshes and renews your body, giving you inspiration and a release from stress.

3. **Share what you're reading.** You *must* have outside inspiration while paying off debt. I can't overstate the role that reading good books and listening to insightful podcasts has had on our journey. Brian and I tend not to read or listen to the same things, but we always benefit from hearing what the other has learned and been inspired by. Spend some time together to discuss what written or spoken words have impacted your souls recently. A list of books that encouraged us during our journey is found on pages 207–209.

4. Talk about your finances. I know this is kind of duh-huh, but you need to meet regularly to discuss budgets, unexpected expenses, and upcoming challenges. You also need to talk about purchases *before* you make them. This will look different for every couple. Brian and I communicate about even a measly ten-dollar purchase when it's a nonbudgeted expense (e.g., not gas, groceries, and other regular bills). Even if your spouse doesn't agree with this principle, you can take the initiative by applying its practice with your own personal purchases. Actions always speak louder than words.

I don't recall either of us weighing in with a "No, that's not a purchase you should make" sort of judgment. However, talking about it ahead of time prevents resentment when one of us brings home a new pair of jeans or a tool. There are no arched eyebrows. There is no *Wonder how much that cost us?* look of despair. Remember: a hot marriage begins with a balanced checkbook, not in a raucous bedroom.

5. Dream big. It's important to talk regularly and with great gusto about the goals you look forward to achieving on the other side of paying off debt! This practice helps you keep your eyes on the prize of the "why" of what you're doing. Brian and I chatted about everything from what we might purchase (or would need to purchase) after we were debt-free, to where we might go, to how we were going to give more and save more on the other side of slaying the debt dragon.

6. Remember your vows. Always keep in mind that your spouse chose *you*! He or she is not out to get you, to ruin your life, or to make you miserable. You are a team, and you LOVE each other. It's easy to begin to think that you're contributing more to the fight against debt than your spouse is. It's easy to let division slip into your marriage. It can be hard to forgive and remember that you walked down the aisle for a reason. The vows you spoke to each other were also promises you made to God. Ask for His wisdom as you seek financial unity in your marriage.

them every time we walk in or out of our home. Both were incredibly important in our journey of paying off $127K. If our house were on fire, I would honestly try to grab them on the way out.

The first is a stack of bills. Every single time we paid off a debt, we wrote the date on the final bill and then clipped it to the other paid-off bills. As the stack grew, we could visually see the change in our lives. We could leaf back through our journey. We could see the totality of our efforts. Pinned to the final document is a little button that says, "To Have More, Desire Less," a paraphrase of a G. K. Chesterton quote.[2] It reminded us that we had all we needed and we would be okay in the midst of battling the debt dragon. Glance at the cover of this book. See all of those papers flying up in the air? Those are the final statements that had been added to the pile on our refrigerator. That photo was taken the day we paid our last debt. We could not recreate the look of relief in our eyes even if we tried. But we picked the papers back up and clipped them to the side of the fridge again, even after that day.

The other document is a single sheet of notebook paper. Its edges are worn, and you can even see the scraggly evidence of where it was once spiral bound. Marked with coffee stains (oops) and scratch math, it is a running total of the debt we paid off. Dates and sums filled the lines and then began to make their way around the edges of the paper. Whenever we felt discouraged, we pulled out that sheet and marveled at the miracle that God had worked in our finances. Things once were so different than they were now.

Other couples may choose to document their path out of debt differently. Maybe you'll draw a giant thermometer and shade in the numbers as you pay off your bills. Maybe you'll pin those bills to a dartboard. Pull out your pencil and mock up a spreadsheet. Or draw a dragon. Whatever it takes for your journey to come alive before you, do it. I promise that if you do, on the days when you want to quit, you'll be able to remember how far you've come and why you still need to soldier on.

Being out of debt means so much more than being free from debtors. You will be able to give away more than you've ever given before. You will live without the worry of whether or not you have enough to "make it." You are endeavoring for more than just getting your finances under control. You are engaged in a soul-shaping process that leads to less malcontent and more gratitude for what you already have, to less fear of scarcity and more peace in Christ.

Debt-Slaying Strategies

✓ Take at least five minutes to pray for financial unity in your marriage right now.

✓ Brainstorm four ways to encourage your spouse.

✓ Focus on what you have instead of letting scarcity steal your joy. List three gifts that remind you that you aren't really "going without" while paying off debt. Breathe words of gratitude for those blessings.

✓ Create a visual that will help fuel your debt-slaying journey.

Chapter 3

STARTING-LINE STRATEGIES

The miracle isn't that I finished. The miracle is that I had the courage to start.
JOHN BINGHAM,
The Courage to Start: A Guide to Running for Your Life

I NEVER THOUGHT I'd be a runner. In college I had friends who ran, and I'll be honest, I thought they were a little crazy. Biking? Sure, that sounded like fun. The occasional aerobics class or kickboxing? I'm in. Joining a pickup game of basketball, hitting the weights, or lobbing a tennis ball (even though I'm horrible with a racquet) all appealed to me. But running? I'll pass. In fact, until a few short years ago, my proudest mantra was "Run only when chased."

Even now, I don't fancy myself as Jesse Owens. I am not an ultra-marathoner by any stretch of the imagination. But I can honestly say that I *do* enjoy running, although it still feels a little wrong to say it out loud. My running shoes tied just so, my favorite playlist locked and loaded, and the worries and responsibilities of my day behind me—there's nothing so freeing as running down my driveway and then crossing the street to the long stretch of sidewalk on my regular route. Even better is the mind-clearing, postrun high when my lungs and soul stretch out, prepared to take on anything the world throws my way.

The more miles I put under my feet while we were slaying the debt dragon, the more I began to see similarities between the daily practice of running and the daily practice of paying off debt. Each time I struggled to motivate myself to run, I was reminded that the starting line for both pursuits is the most difficult to cross. Once my legs get into motion, there's no stopping my run. However, the most difficult step for me, as I'm guessing it is for most people, is actually digging out my running shoes. Remaining on the couch? It's so much more comfortable. It's easier. It's softer. It's warmer. It's effortless. For most of us, staying in one place always seems more natural than putting our bodies in motion.

The same is true of our finances. It is always easier to keep spending mindlessly and giving in to our own (or our kids') whims, no matter the cost. It's always easier to stay on the couch, physically or metaphorically. It's always easier to stay well behind the starting line. If we actually find the motivation to put our body or our debt-reducing plan into motion, we're also bound to feel pain. That's because strengthening ourselves physically or financially requires first tearing and then rebuilding muscle.

> Strengthening ourselves physically or financially requires first tearing and then rebuilding muscle.

I promise I'm not trying to be Debbie Downer. The last thing I would ever want to do is discourage you. In fact, I'm probably not even telling you something you don't already know. I just want to gently remind you that reducing your debt—like anything with long-term health benefits—needs to be done purposefully, not haphazardly. Every successful venture begins with a strategy. In this chapter, I'd like to present you with some ideas on how to start attacking your own debt dragon. I'd also like to offer some encouragement to move beyond those strategies and put your plan into motion.

Name It . . . Then Kill It

Once the two of you are unified and excited to begin the battle together, your next action step might seem a wee bit—how shall I say it?—unconventional. Yet, I believe this essential step has the power to draw you even closer together: you need to give your debt a name. Here's why.

Names have power. When someone mispronounces our name (it happens to me often), our whole attitude can shift. We are insulted when someone has forgotten our name. We wrap our ears around soothing voices who call our names. Speaking the name of someone we love can make our heart skip a beat.

I've named teddy bears. I've named cars. (Long live Cami the Camaro!) I've named imaginary friends. I've named children. I've named ministries. Each time, I have taken great care in bestowing a name because it can speak volumes about the bearer and even more about the namer.

....

Student Loan's Eviction Notice   ○○○
Adapted from a January 2012 blog post

Dear Evil Sorceress Student Loan,

You've lived with us for a very long time.

You were there when we got engaged. You were there when we graduated from college. You stood up with us at the wedding (even though no one invited you to do that).

You came along on the honeymoon over twelve years ago (that

was totally awkward). You dwelled in our first two apartments, keeping us from truly ever having any time alone as newlyweds.

You were there for the birth of the Princess Eldest and kept us from loving her in the ways we wanted to love her (and from paying her hospital bills as quickly as we would have liked, too).

You kept us from doing things that we longed to do—saving for retirement, starting college funds, giving when we saw a need, having regular date nights, going on vacation, and even buying things we needed. (Have you seen our towels lately? Holy holey, Batman.)

Nearly four years ago, right after the Princess Youngest was born, your vacant ugly stare came at us in the form of a very large number—over $80K. We wanted you gone. But you were *so* huge that we had no idea where to begin. Your younger and much thinner student loan sister was one of the first to receive her eviction notice in July 2008. Your cousins—medical debt, car loan debt, furniture loan debt, small loan debt, and credit card debt—all followed suit thereafter. Since February 2010 we have watched you—and you alone—slowly but surely dwindle. Now, you number only four digits instead of six, and by our best estimates, in about four months you'll need to leave our house—FOREVER.

You are certainly not welcome back. Ever. Consider yourself forewarned. You have more than overstayed your welcome.

And you will never plant your evil claws into our two sweet little girls. Their college educations will be financed by your arch nemesis—the heroic and oh-so-brave CA$H.

Your days are numbered.

Pack your bags. We're coming for you.

The King and Queen of Free

....

While I can't nail down the exact date when Brian and I began referring to our debt as "the dragon," personifying our financial obligations became one of the most powerful strategies for getting our finances under control.

Nameless, a force in your life remains neutral. You approach it with a disinterested spirit. Give your debt a name, and it becomes much, much more personal. If you want victory over debt, you must make the battle personal.

Society wants to make you think that debt is neutral—even natural.

That it's not that big of a deal.
That it's the only way to get what you want.
That everyone else has debt.
That you can coexist peacefully.

This was certainly the case for my friend Luke. He was told during college that without using credit, he wouldn't be able to get a job after graduation. Ten years later, Luke is happily married and has two sweet little boys, but his family is still paying for the items purchased on credit when he was in college. My friend Nickole was a college freshman when she was convinced it was a good idea for her to sign up for a credit card. In fact, if she did, she would receive a *free* T-shirt. That T-shirt resulted in over $1,000 in debt by her junior year. Perhaps it wasn't free after all. Then there's Stacey, who was told that going to college required debt. Students either took out student loans or they didn't go. She wishes someone

> If you want victory over debt, you must make the battle personal.

had told her what $40,000 per year would look like as a monthly payment after she graduated. Society tells us that jobs, free T-shirts, and a college education are available only to those with debt.

All of the above are lies.

When we wake up from the lies of the status quo and the enemy of our souls, we realize many truths about debt. Debt is a disease. Debt is your enemy. Debt wants to destroy you. Debt wants to kill your marriage. Debt wants to wreck your children. Debt wants to control your day-to-day purchases. Debt wants to steal your joy. Debt wants to damage your health. Above all else, debt wants to keep you from being generous.

Doesn't that make you mad? Not really? Okay, let me try again. Let's replace the word *debt* with *Fred Johnson*.

Fred Johnson is a disease. Fred Johnson is your enemy. Fred Johnson wants to destroy you. Fred Johnson wants to kill your marriage. Fred Johnson wants to wreck your children. Fred Johnson wants to control your day-to-day purchases. Fred Johnson wants to steal your joy. Fred Johnson wants to damage your health. Above all else, Fred Johnson wants to keep you from being generous.

Who's ready to take to the streets and run Fred Johnson's underwear up a flagpole while screaming "FRREEDDOMM!" *Braveheart* style?[1] Fred Johnson has got one coming. Someone needs to knock out that guy's teeth. No one messes with your family. How dare the interloper Fred Johnson meddle in your marriage? And who is Fred Johnson to tell you how much you can give or how you should live your life?[2]

The small act of personifying your debt makes your soul cry out, *That's not right! This bully must be stopped!*

Until you realize that debt is your enemy, you won't truly be angry enough at your situation to make significant change. When Brian and I zeroed in on debt *really* being our enemy? That's when we began to gain traction. Monthly balances don't seem like evil villains threatening to kill, steal, and destroy you. But that's precisely what they are. Once we'd identified the debt dragon that was threatening our family, Brian and I embarked on a quest to slay that beast, to dislodge its talons from our finances, to remove its presence from our marriage, and to keep it from stealing the treasures of our children, our checkbook, and our souls.

Identifying debt as our enemy was most useful in the area of our marriage. Never in nine years of marriage had we had a knock-down,

QUICK WAYS TO START BUILDING AN EMERGENCY FUND

Getting out of debt is difficult if you keep adding to it. Yet life is full of costly surprises—like overflowing washing machines, emergency room visits, and smoking car engines. That's why building an emergency fund is so critical. While setting aside enough cash to cover several months of living expenses may seem daunting, Brian and I discovered some simple ways to start building the fund fast.

- Roll your change and exchange it for cash at your bank—or let a self-service coin machine do the sorting for you. (Keep in mind, though, that machines require a processing fee.)

- Get several estimates on your broken or unused jewelry from retailers who buy gold; sell to the highest reputable bidder.

- Sell items from your home on Facebook; search for local Facebook groups that specialize in selling home goods and cross-promote your items there.

- Pick up an extra job—like babysitting, delivering pizza, mowing lawns, or pet sitting—that requires no financial investment and leads to a quick paycheck.

- At the grocery store, use cash only.

- Commit to packing and taking your lunch to work daily.

- Go without eating at restaurants for thirty days.

- Take a six-month break from attending—or at least purchasing from—home party sales.

- Talk with family members and close friends about giving up gift-giving between adults during the holidays and on birthdays.

drag-out fight (what a horrible expression!) about money. But as I mentioned in chapter 1, we had begun to passively-aggressively pick apart many of each other's purchases.

Did you really need that?
You spent how much?
Can we afford that?

You see, getting into debt . . . that can tear a marriage apart. Make you fight. Make you resentful. Make you stop communicating. Make you annoyed at every single penny spent by your spouse. Debt leads to tension. It can overwhelm you both, causing you to be angry at each other for reasons you can't vocalize, or maybe even for no reason at all.

Money (or the lack thereof) makes couples crazy. More divorces begin from problems with money than any other issue.[3] In his work as an attorney, Brian has seen how debt often leads couples to abandon their vows and convinces them to see divorce as the only option.

Personifying debt was one way Brian and I were able to come together to begin fighting a battle against our common foe—not against each other. That strategy allowed us to drop the passive-aggressive accusations and focus on what truly mattered. Getting out of debt together? We now had a common enemy. One we would fight together. That it would take both of us to conquer. Our shared adversary pitted the two of us against the world, binding our hearts together.

Paying off $127K+ in debt with the King of Free made me feel like we were spies, going into hostile territory where our enemy the debt dragon wanted to plunder every single thing we held dear. But we battled that dragon *together*. We fought back-to-back with our weapons drawn. Granted, our weapons were not guns or even swords, but a strong budget, coupons, extra jobs, intentionality, patience, contentment, focus, faith, intensity, and a whole lot of prayer. We found safety and serenity in each other's arms every day after fierce battle, knowing that, with God's help, together we *could* defeat the dragon.

We all need someone to have our back when we're slaying debt. If you're single, that might be your parents or close friend. It might be a trusted roommate or mentor. Certainly, none of us was meant to live this life in isolation, to travel or fight on our own. The debt dragon longs for you to be and feel alone in your pursuit. He knows that when you're alone, you're more vulnerable and likely to give up.

To avoid those sneaky and despicable tactics of your enemy, you're going to have to ask for help. Who knows your heart, friend? Who longs to see you win (with money and in life)? Who can you count on to walk with you through a difficult journey?

Choose wisely. Don't settle for just anyone. Instead, find a co-battler who understands the "why" of your decision to pay off your debt and is willing to stand by you in the most difficult of days. Don't hesitate. Invite that individual into your story now. Be humble. Acknowledge your inability to go it alone. If no one comes to mind immediately, I encourage you to ask God to bring someone

Naming your debt can annihilate that unspoken and unidentifiable fear that it brings into your life.

across your path. You just might be surprised who becomes your greatest ally in slaying this enemy. Am I saying that you must have a debt dragon of your own? Well, yes and no. Your debt doesn't have to be a dragon. You can name it Larry. You can name it Moe. You can name it Fred Johnson. But give it a name, and then go all Rocky Balboa on that beast. Naming your debt can annihilate that unspoken and unidentifiable fear that it brings into your life. You can focus on why you must remove it and discover the drive you need to pay it off, improving your financial fiefdom.

Wait, What's *Your* Name Again?

Giving your debt a name can be empowering. But you can also draw strength from the names God gives you.

Did you know that God is in the naming and renaming business? Throughout the Bible, God took the time to give new names to those He called. Abram became Abraham. Sarai became Sarah. Jacob's name change was more drastic. He had to change the wording on his "Hello, My Name Is" tag to Israel. Simon received his new name, Peter, from Jesus Himself. Perhaps most confusing of all, Saul dropped the *S* and added a *P* to become Paul. (Obviously, God never changed anyone's name to Fred Johnson.)

With each name change, God began writing a new story with His children's lives. God began calling Abram his new name, Abraham—which means "Father of Many Nations"—when he was nearly a century old and before he had a single child. The name Peter means "rock." Only Christ would select such a stalwart moniker for a man who would both cut off someone's ear in an attempt to protect Jesus and then deny ever even knowing Him due to his fear of the unknown.

God wants you to learn your *true* name—discovering who you truly are made to be—during your quest to pay off debt. However, there are a few things I know about how God has already "named" you in the midst of your debt-slaying journey.

> **Paying off debt isn't complex; it's just not easy.**

He has named you intelligent enough to pay off debt.

God knows that you have what it takes to fight and win this battle. You have the smarts. It doesn't take an academic genius to pay off debt. Honestly, it really isn't *that* complex. Spend less than you make so you can whack away incrementally at the debt dragon with all you've got. It's not exactly an algebraic formula reserved only for financial whizzes. Indeed, *paying off debt isn't complex; it's just not easy.* You don't need a graduate degree, a fancy calculator, or a smarty-pants cap and gown. You are smart enough already. God has given you all you need.

He has named you capable enough to pay off debt.

We often confuse the ability to pay off debt with our financial know-how or how "good" we are with money. Most likely, that's an easy out—an excuse to keep doing the things we're doing in the way we're doing them without guilt or repercussions (ouch).

But I'd like to claim a truth that you may not yet know in this debt-slaying journey. Everything you need to pay off all of your debt is already in your possession. Don't go running through your house looking for a boatload of cash that would settle all of your accounts today. That comes only with time. What is in your possession are the discipline and tools it takes to be intentional with your finances.

Honestly. If you have ever

- ○ baked a cake, you have what it takes.
- ○ run a mile, you have what it takes.
- ○ knitted a scarf, you have what it takes.
- ○ learned to play a musical instrument, you have what it takes.
- ○ given birth to a child, you have what it takes.
- ○ homeschooled, you *definitely* have what it takes.
- ○ applied for and gotten a job, you have what it takes.
- ○ remained married for more than a year (or ten or forty or more), you have what it takes.
- ○ endeavored to become healthier, you have what it takes.
- ○ learned to read (ha! got all of you on that one), you have what it takes.

Maybe you're thinking, *But those accomplishments have nothing to do with money.* Wrong. Each of them takes a specific skill set, but more than that, each requires discipline. And if you've done any of them? I *know* you can pay off all of your debt.

You see, the tools required to succeed in any of the above categories are transferable. The gifts and stick-to-it-iveness necessary to defeat debt may feel dormant in your soul, but they remain a part of who you are. You already have all you need to pay off all of your debt.

God has named you brave enough to pay off your debt.

Fear. At some point it paralyzes us all. I used to rush into bed after switching off the lights, sure that somehow my magic comforter would protect me from the evils that lurked in the dark. Or at least make me invisible. (Okay, so I still practice that running start when the King of Free isn't home. What's up with that reasoning? While he's certainly my knight in shining armor, he's not a ninja.)

We all have fears and we *all* struggle with them. The dark, heights, spiders, public speaking, flying, snakes, or clowns. But probably the most universal of all fears is failure.

I've found that many money-saving lords and ladies seeking to slay debt and gain freedom struggle with this fear more than any other. And if they speak into existence their intention to dig their way out of deep debt, then the possibility of failure looms in the dark and indiscriminate distance. What if everyone finds out? What if they can't finish the task? What if they fail?

So they never even try.

It's too hard.
Life will be boring.
We just can't do it.
We won't have any fun.
It's too much of a sacrifice.
We've tried so many times before.

It's not that they are sissies. It's just that becoming debt-free requires change, and that change often brings fear. Doing something different is scary. Getting out of debt is different. Getting out of debt is scary.

In the beginning of our family's journey, the balance sheet dripped a scary red. The path seemed impossible and the challenges insurmountable. Failure was imminent. The debt dragon had very large teeth and snarled with every step we took toward it.

But God gave us the courage to take on what we thought was absolutely absurd. "Be strong and courageous. Do not be afraid; do not be discouraged, for the LORD your God will be with you wherever you go."[4] God's words to Joshua became our battle cry. On the other side of freedom, I now question why that dragon ever looked so scary compared to our God. Surely, *nothing* is impossible for Him.

At some point you have to ask yourself if fear has more value than freedom in your life. Is it better to bow at the feet of fear or to seek true freedom?

> **You have to ask yourself if fear has more value than freedom in your life.**

Still scared? Believe it or not, that's *good news*. In the Bible, often the first thing out of God's mouth or the mouths of His messengers was "Do not be afraid." When individuals were faced with His presence or had to respond to His calling for their lives, God consistently quelled their fears with a "fear not." Want to call my bluff? Here are a few passages that illustrate this fact.[5]

God spoke to Israel in a vision at night and said, "Jacob! Jacob!"

"Here I am," he replied.

"I am God, the God of your father," he said. "*Do not be afraid* to go down to Egypt, for I will make you into a great nation there. I will go down to Egypt with you, and I will surely bring you back again. And Joseph's own hand will close your eyes."

GENESIS 46:2-4, NIV

The LORD said to me, "Do not say, 'I am a youth,' because everywhere I send you, you shall go, and all that I command you, you shall speak. *Do not be afraid of them*, for I am with you to deliver you," declares the LORD.

JEREMIAH 1:7-8, NASB

Mary was greatly troubled at his words and wondered what kind of greeting this might be. But the angel said to her, "*Do not be afraid*, Mary; you have found favor with God. You will conceive and give birth to a son, and you are to call him Jesus."

LUKE 1:29-31, NIV

An angel of the Lord suddenly stood before them, and the glory of the Lord shone around them; and they were terribly frightened. But the angel said to them, "*Do not be afraid*; for behold, I bring you good news of great joy which will be for all the people; for today in the city of David there has been born for you a Savior, who is Christ the Lord."

LUKE 2:9-11, NASB

The angel said to the women, "*Do not be afraid*, for I know that you are looking for Jesus, who was crucified. He is not here; he has risen, just as he said. Come and see the place where he lay."

MATTHEW 28:5-6, NIV

DEBT-SLAYING HERO

CHRISTOPHER, 37 | **PAID OFF $90,000**

For years after earning both college and graduate degrees, Christopher made only the minimum payments on his student loans, putting any extra cash he made into investments. As a result, the interest continued to accrue on those loans. In 2008, when the stock market dropped, he realized that most of his hard-earned dollars had vanished while his massive student loan debt had continued to grow. He immediately began to redirect his efforts.

Why slay the debt dragon?

After catching Dave Ramsey's show on the radio during his daily commute, Christopher's interest was piqued. With his investments down the tubes and his debt increasing daily, was there actually a way out for him? Hearing of others' success provided all the motivation he needed to launch his journey.

What surprised him the most?

Christopher was surprised to learn just how devastatingly debt can sabotage the creation of wealth. "Every year I paid out thousands of dollars in interest alone. Since paying off my debt, I have again started investing in the market (albeit a bit more conservatively this time)." After carefully tracking his net worth each year since slaying his debt dragon, Christopher has been shocked at how quickly his net worth has grown now that he's not paying out so much to interest each year.

Where did he find joy in the journey?

Christopher's grand total was comprised of student loans and a car. After paying off the car, he started in on the student loans, tackling the smallest first and moving up toward the biggest debt. "I gained a great sense of satisfaction by paying off each balance, and then increasing the amount I paid toward the next biggest balance. Since my loans were split between a few different lenders, I felt like I was making a lot of progress with each new balance being fully paid."

How did he celebrate?

After a well-deserved steak dinner at a local high-end restaurant, Christopher celebrated by directing what would have been his next student loan payment of $1,300 into his retirement account.

What was most challenging?

Even though the starting balance was $90,000, Christopher dove into the challenge with great gusto. It was a journey that took four years. Ironically, after paying off about two-thirds of his debt, fatigue set in. "Once my balance was down to around $30,000, I had the most difficulty staying focused on repayment."

His encouragement and advice for you

Having like-minded travelers on your debt-slaying journey is essential. Christopher encourages you to surround yourself with people who have a similar attitude toward debt. "Many of my friends joined me and decided to become debt-free also. Hearing their stories motivated me to continue on my own path. Also, there is less temptation when all of your friends are more concerned with paying off debt than spending money." Just as vital in Christopher's journey was setting bite-size goals. After achieving these smaller monthly goals within his greater debt-slaying journey, Christopher would reward himself with a minor splurge—like a lunch or dinner out with friends.

If you're scared to begin a debt-slaying journey, it means that God is very near. His calling is very real, and He wants to make His presence known to you.

Receive your true name. Realize that God is bigger than your fears and that *He is near*. Then, name your debt and kill it.

Your Very Personal Battle Plan

Oh, how I wish that merely naming your debt was enough to eliminate it. Oh, how I wish that you could call it what it is, realize what God can do through you, and then be debt-free. But alas, a name alone won't pay it off. Naming it is not enough to move you from "I owe" to true freedom. To slay your debt dragon, you must have a battle plan. You must calculate your attack. While realizing you have a true enemy will motivate your gut and soul in new ways, there has to be a "next step" in order to move from fantasy to reality.

Early on, I would literally dream about miraculously receiving a check for the *exact* amount we owed. What fun it would be to tell the story of how God provided for us to the exact penny. It remained a dream that never came true. But God did provide. He provided additional income through long hours and extra jobs. He provided through bonuses, each penny designated toward paying off debt. (At one point midway through our journey, the King of Free calculated how many flat screens we could have purchased using the money we put toward paying off debt. Short answer? An entire football field of TVs.) God tailored His provision for us, spaced out over time so that we could learn the lessons He knew we needed to learn.

For over twenty years, Dave Ramsey has been counseling people on how to get out (or even better, how to stay out) of debt. So it's little wonder that whenever the word "debt-free" rolls out of my mouth, someone asks whether we followed Dave Ramsey's plan. (Side note: How ridiculously awesome would it be for *your* name to be so synonymous with financial freedom that people would immediately see your face whenever someone said "debt-free" in any context?) The short answer is yes, we did follow Dave's "Baby Step" plan in our approach to paying off debt.[6] As I mentioned before, *The Total Money Makeover* was the book that launched our journey.

The longer answer is that we were intentional about owning the process and applying our own unique spin to paying off debt. Hence the whole debt dragon thing. If you're to be successful at slaying the debt dragon, you can't simply adopt someone else's plan (even mine) for your finances. You need to sit down and think about what most motivates you. You need to set goals that are uniquely designed for your family. You need to be a leader, not a follower, when it comes to your money. You should definitely read great books filled with wisdom about money. You should definitely listen to people who have been successful in their pursuits to pay off debt. You should definitely spend every single second of free time you have researching ways to reduce your spending and increase your income. What you definitely *shouldn't* do is let a good plan remain lifeless. Bring your own gifts, imagination, and grit to it.

Oddly enough, we never took Financial Peace University (FPU), the multiweek course in which Dave breaks down his philosophy and moves participants through a number of set exercises to understand the process. That's not to knock it—many people have found that it offers the step-by-step guidelines they need. It's just that once Brian and I began paying off debt, we were *too cheap* to pay for the course. Instead, we listened to Dave on the radio and podcasts. I used to refer to his radio show as my own personal debtor version of AA. Daily, Dave and I would have "meetings" from 12 to 3 p.m., when our local radio station broadcast the show. In fact, I tuned in so often that my daughters could answer the questions asked by callers because they had heard Dave's responses to similar questions so many times before. There is nothing funnier than hearing a seven-year-old girl yelling,

"No, that would be *stupid!*" to someone calling to ask whether he should pull a five-figure loan to buy equipment for his business.

As much as we are incredibly grateful for the ways that Dave Ramsey's words changed the course and quality of our lives, we often joke, "We love Dave Ramsey, but we worship Jesus." Before you push back immediately (especially if you are Dave Ramsey—please say, yes, you *are* Dave Ramsey and are reading these words because that would be *epic*), understand that I am not demeaning someone else's work at all. There is an age-old temptation to create idols out of those we admire, crediting them with the work that only God can do. God certainly works through humanity, but let's not focus energy on heaping praise upon people rather than the God who works through people.

Unfortunately, I know some people who have become "Ramsey-heads" and enjoy Dave's content as mere entertainment, but who refuse to change their financial practices. These people have not been successful in paying off debt. But the people I know who have gone beyond being hearers of the word and have become doers, applying their own gifts and passion to the process, have paid off astronomical amounts. I urge you, like them, to incorporate sound financial principles with your God-given gifts and dreams for your finances. Dave Ramsey did not write a check to pay off all of our debt. He's not going to write a check like that for you, either. You must move beyond strategies and theories to make your debt-slaying journey your own.

Back in April 2008, Brian and I focused first on the initial baby steps in Ramsey's plan, beginning with saving $1,000 for an emergency fund—which we were able to do, thanks to a tax refund. We then adjusted our withholdings so we wouldn't receive tax refunds in the future. It meant a wee bit of sadness the next spring when we didn't get a refund, but it also meant an extra $100 per month that we could use to take the second baby step and begin paying off our debt.

Now, at first glance, this second baby step doesn't seem logical because it advises you to pay off your debts from smallest to largest, regardless of interest rate. Almost every time I share the debt snowball philosophy at speaking engagements, someone argues with me about the amount of interest you will end up paying if you eliminate debt in this sequence.

Can I be straight with you? We weren't so great at math. If we were, we would never have racked up $127K of debt in the first place. You see, personal finance has less to do with numbers than it does with personal behavior and discipline. The reason the debt snowball was so effective for us was that we quickly began to see the results of our efforts. In the past, when we had tried to pay off the highest-interest debt first, we would make minor progress but then become discouraged because we never seemed to make enough headway. It was very easy to give up because we weren't making any progress, or at least it didn't "feel" like we were.

Eliminating a small debt quickly allowed us to put that regular payment amount toward the next biggest debt. We had "found" extra money that we didn't need for the purposes of living to heap upon the next debt in line, giving us more traction, which yielded more success. The momentum and emotions that accompany success are absolutely addictive. We became driven to find more ways to scale back our lifestyle, save money, and bring in extra income because we now knew that dragons could be beaten. We rolled the debt snowball along fairly quickly during the first fifteen months.

Life is full of surprises, which meant that sometimes we had to pause our debt repayment efforts so we could rebuild our emergency fund. I can't count the number of times that this account was emptied as we were paying off our debt. Whenever we had to pay for some unexpected large expense—a root canal, braces, a new water heater, or car repairs—we dipped into the emergency fund. Our priority then became rebuilding that emergency account, even though it was quite frustrating to have to put less toward paying off debt. We became creative in finding ways to replenish the fund: we dug change out of every corner of our house and car, pawned jewelry, sold books, and put every monetary gift we received (aka birthday money from our parents) toward it.

Before we knew it, we had only two debts remaining. Granted, they made up about $105K of the $127K and would take *years* longer than the smaller debts to pay off, but we had gained momentum by paying off the smaller debts, leaving us with a larger sword with which to jab at the dragon.

An Open Letter to My Nemesis
Adapted from two blog posts written by the King of Free in 2008

Early in our debt-slaying journey, the King of Free put the Debt Dragon on notice. He often doesn't capitalize words (he thinks he is e. e. cummings), and he uses slang, along with odd and obscure pop culture references. You might have to use Google or ask your spouse if they know what he's talking about. But I think you'll be amused by his take—and might even get some ideas on how to take on debt yourself.

Dear Debt Dragon:

- My primary vehicle is a truck with over 215K miles. To exit, I must put down the driver's side window and open the door from the outside. Often the window is already down because the air conditioning is inoperable. While AC would be nice, I have no desire for a new vehicle.
- We recently gave up cable. Killin' my brain cells anyway.
- We ditched the rental water softener. Don't think it ever worked.
- I eat oatmeal for breakfast just about every day, less than 20 cents' worth of yum.
- We garden. mmmm, nature.
- I have three jobs. I'd take a fourth.
- We stay out of the mall. Don't wanna know what it is that i must have.

- We don't have a microwave. Many sing legend of the Queen's stovetop popcorn.
- We don't go to the movies. Netflix. Snuggle. Queen.
- We don't drink pop. The water from my congreenient Brita pitcher is sublime.
- No expensive hobbies. I "do not" something.
- We coupon. It's a verb the way the Queen does it.
- You knocked me down. I got up.
- Nixed the expensive gym membership. Local church is cleaner and on the cheap.
- I sold baseball cards and books. Got more to sell.
- Sold old jewelry too.

I no longer just march to the beat of a different drummer. I *am* the different drummer.

There is a crowd. A movement of people marching to this new beat who are sick of your shenanigans. This beat is a prelude to your demise. A symphony of destruction. I ain't alone, you slimy lizard. We're coming for you. One small change at a time. We're coming for you.

yours truly,
King of Free

Start Small: Crazy Comes in Phases

Certainly you have to be a little crazy to successfully pay off debt, but your wackiness must come in phases. Drastic crazy is unsustainable. The intense actions we took in year four, during the final stages of our battle with the debt dragon, would never have flown in year one. In fact, I would more than likely have told you those were changes only bizarre people would make. For instance, during the last six to nine months of our journey, we gave up eating meat to save more money to fuel the final battle. In year one, this certainly would have smacked of wacky to me. I must have gotten much better at wearing my crazy on my sleeve as our journey progressed. Either that or the more we whacked away at the debt dragon, the more I was willing to sacrifice for a greater goal, no matter how off the wall it appeared to the outside world.

In *The 2 Degree Difference*, John Trent explains why big solutions rarely solve big problems.[7] Instead, small changes over a long period of time tend to yield a greater result. Whether pursuing a more active lifestyle, a new method of discipline for our children, changes in our finances, or changes in nutrition, we usually fail when we bite off more than we can chew. A 180-degree change will almost always ensure failure, while two-degree changes bring with them success.

For instance, say you are a die-hard Diet Coke drinker, downing four or five giant servings per day. You wake up one morning and declare to the universe, "For as long as I live, nevermore shall I partake in such revelry again. Sayonora, my aspartame-y, bubbly friend. You are no longer welcome here." My guess is that by the end of the week, you would be sitting in the middle of your living room. At your feet would be a shredded twenty-four-pack that appeared to have been ripped apart by a feral animal. All around you would be dozens of cans, each drained of every drop. You'd have a wild look in your eyes as you rocked back and forth, hair in a matted mess, humming the newest Taylor Swift jingle.

You, sweet Diet Coke–drinking friend, would have made too drastic a change, one that was unsustainable.

In chapters 5 through 8, I share many of the money-saving tips that Brian and I used when we were slaying our debt dragon—and which we continue to follow today even though we're debt-free. I think you'll find some helpful ideas to try right away, but I don't expect you to look at those as your marching orders for tomorrow, or even next week. Our family certainly didn't make all of these changes overnight. Many of our lifestyle modifications were small in nature and were made gradually, one at a time.

Keep in mind, it took four *years* of our lives to pay off such an enormous sum. Think about all that can happen in four years. You can earn a high school diploma or gain a medical degree. The small modifications we put into place seemed inconsequential at first glance, but over those days, weeks, months, and years, they truly added up.

Begin thinking of simple, manageable steps to take when it comes to your finances. Keep a small change in place for thirty days—the time estimated to create a habit—and then look for another small change that you can implement. A little bit over a long period of time yields a great reward. A landslide of change usually results in an enormous mess.

Just Do It!

Theories and debt-elimination strategies are certainly required for those who want to be successful in paying off all of their debt. No one gets anywhere without a plan or a road map. However, beware of enveloping yourself in good intentions, looking for the perfect system or the absolute best method of approach. Spoiler: there are more ways than one to pay off all your liabilities. I don't keep a financial top secret in a vault buried beneath the floorboards of our home. I can attest to the fact that the method we used was successful. If it had remained a strategy in name but not in action, we would still be stretched beyond our limits and a complete wreck—financially, emotionally, and spiritually.

Financial freedom and transformation doesn't come simply because you long for it. Here's the thing: Let's say you have all you need to train to run a marathon—the shoes, a great playlist, a training schedule, even a fancy heart-rate monitor. Yet if you remain on the couch at home eating Ding Dongs, you're never going to make it out the front door, let alone 26.2 miles down the road.

At some point you have to lace up your shoes and put your feet to the pavement. It's the same with your debt: you *must* take action. It will require sacrifice on your part. It will require hard work. The days will feel long. Just as if you were running a race, you might sweat or even cry. Some days, you will feel like giving up. Persist anyway.

If you can get over the little bumps in the road, victory looms in the distance. It may feel unreachable at times, I know, but you can get there. Can I leave you with some inspiration from the Bible?

Do you see what this means—all these pioneers who blazed the way, all these veterans cheering us on? It means we'd better get on with it. Strip down, start running—and never quit! No extra spiritual fat, no parasitic sins. Keep your eyes on *Jesus*, who both began and finished this race we're in. Study how he did it. Because he never lost sight of where he was headed—that exhilarating finish in and with God—he could put up with anything along the way: Cross, shame, whatever. And now he's *there*, in the place of honor, right alongside God. When you find yourselves flagging in your faith, go over that story again, item by item, that long litany of hostility he plowed through. *That* will shoot adrenaline into your souls!

HEBREWS 12:1-3 (italics in the original)

Can you see why I love the analogy between running and debt slaying so much? Of course, I'm far from the first person to make the comparison. I'm not a professional runner. My times are mediocre, and I've never run a marathon before. My training schedules can be on-again, off-again in nature. Yet even when I've been the most consistent about running, those first two miles are *always* the hardest. My lungs burn, my legs feel creaky, and I'm kind of cranky. When you first start your debt-slaying journey, it probably won't feel good. You might be a little winded and cranky too. But don't give up, even if you're sore and convinced you'll never make it to the finish line.

Looking back over the marathon Brian and I ran to pay off our debt, I can honestly say that every moment of self-doubt, every stinking sacrifice, every time I had to turn down something fun because "we couldn't afford it" pales in comparison to the sense of freedom I feel today. So never forget: the pain of the first few miles on your race to financial freedom will be worth enduring for the joy you feel on your final sprint to the finish.

Debt-Slaying Strategies

✓ Brainstorm a list of potential names for your debt. Once you settle on one you like, try it out with the following statements.

- Watch out, _____; I'm coming for you.

- Enough of your lies and misgivings, _____!

- You will not claim my marriage, my joy, my children, or my ability to give, _____.

✓ List four habits or hobbies you've mastered which required intentionality and discipline. Contemplate how those skills might be transferable in your journey of slaying the debt dragon.

✓ If you don't already have an emergency fund, begin saving for one. Look at the kick-starter, money-saving ideas in the sidebar on page 37. Name one idea from there—or brainstorm one of your own ideas—that you will implement this week so you have more money to put toward an emergency fund or paying down your debts.

Chapter 4

BUDGETS ARE YOUR BATTLE-AX

The general who wins the battle makes many calculations in his temple before the battle is fought. The general who loses makes but few calculations beforehand.

SUN TZU

TOWARD THE END of our debt-slaying journey, I had an enlightening encounter that has forever changed the way I view paying off debt. My eureka wasn't found in a textbook or even a sermon. It was found in the mundane simplicity of everyday life. I was running errands, which included a quick trip to pick up a prescription at my local superstore. I planned to zip in and zip right back out. But on my way to the pharmacy, my eyes wandered to Christmas clearance items in a center aisle.

I love a good bargain—always have, always will—so the "90 Percent Off" sign drew me in like a tractor beam. Almost immediately my eyes zeroed in on a stack of cherry-red placemats that had been marked down to nineteen cents each.

Some people spend their lives devoted to curing cancer. Some people design skyscrapers. Some people are naturally inclined toward relieving suffering. Apparently my spiritual gifts include identifying an amazing deal in under fifteen seconds. Did I mention how well those placemats would match our kitchen, which is red and yellow? On top of that, they were plastic—easy to clean and great for the princesses! And four placemats could be mine, all for less than eighty cents!

What should I do? Alas, I am not the Queen of Really Cheap—I am the Queen of Free. And even though I'd spend under a dollar, I knew that, technically, this was an "extra" sort of purchase. We were literally putting every extra penny we had toward finishing the race of paying off debt. I already had perfectly good placemats that I loved. Bottom line: those placemats were a "want"—something I'd buy on impulse—not any sort of need. I mean, c'mon, no one really needs placemats, right? My world wasn't going to crash and burn without them.

Even though it may sound utterly ridiculous, I walked away without the nineteen-cent steal of a deal. Here's when my epiphany about our journey locked in. I knew that if I could say no to nineteen cents, I could also say no to $1.90 or $19 or $190 or even $1,900. It's all the same.

> Saying no is challenging, but it is the most successful way to pay off debt.

Saying no is challenging, but it is the most successful way to pay off debt. Guess what? I was just fine without those placemats. And as I noted on my blog later that night, we were seventy-six cents closer to paying off our last student loan payment because of that decision.

Once again, paying off debt is not complex; it's just not easy.

Writing It Down

I've never met anyone pursuing an extraordinary goal who didn't have a written plan. Rarely does someone stumble into greatness. Whether it's training for an Ironman Triathlon or starting a business, the path

DEBT-SLAYING DUO

**DANIEL AND EMILY, BOTH 29
PARENTS OF DALLAS, 5** | **PAID OFF $91,000**

How I wish Brian and I had caught the vision to get out of debt when we were in our midtwenties like Daniel and Emily! With so much of their lives ahead of them as a young married couple, they won't face the same struggles many families overwhelmed with debt experience. Instead, they can focus on building a future for their son, Dallas, and enjoy the many gifts God has blessed their family with.

Why slay the debt dragon?
Perhaps like you, Daniel and Emily were inspired by a friend's family who had also begun paying off debt. That inspiration quickly turned into a fire, fueling them to slay their own personal debt dragon. This young family also dreamed of financial freedom for their young son. Once they began seriously pursuing their goal, it took only twenty-five months for Daniel and Emily to pay off their $91,000 obligation.

What surprised them most about paying off debt?
The whole concept of being debt-free and paying with cash seemed like common sense for Daniel and Emily. Like many people, they had simply never stopped to contemplate the possibility of a life without debt. This family was also pleasantly surprised at how quickly they could pay down their balance when they had a clear plan for their money. Strengthened by being on the same page financially, Daniel and Emily delighted in their marriage. Fighting about money became a thing of the past as they began communicating more clearly and working together.

What was most challenging?

Midway through their journey, Daniel and Emily felt a call to expand their family—only to face the pressures of infertility. The emotional and financial challenges of battling two enemies at once was wearisome. Keeping their eyes focused on God's plan for their finances helped them both gather strength and courage during a heart-wrenching experience. Thankfully, they were able to pay cash for medical treatments and avoid going further into the red.

How did they celebrate?

Like so many others, Daniel and Emily decided to make a "Debt-free!" scream on Dave Ramsey's radio show part of their celebration. They enjoyed the opportunity to share their story with friends and family who listened in to cheer with them. The chance to thank Dave was high on their priority list too.

Their encouragement and advice for you

Today is your best day to begin paying off debt. Daniel and Emily don't want you to hesitate: "Just do it! What do you have to lose? Nothing. What do you have to gain? Everything." Feeling frustrated or weary about where you are financially? Even if you have already established a budget, Daniel and Emily recommend you comb through it again to see what other adjustments you might make. It can feel like getting a raise when you reexamine where you can find additional dollars. This wise couple adds, "Anything worth doing takes time, effort, and struggle. Don't give up."

How has paying off debt changed their marriage?

Daniel and Emily say that paying off debt brought a complete paradigm shift in how they view money within their marriage. Having a common goal brought purpose and intentionality to their finances while bringing their hearts closer together, which, they say, "enabled us to achieve true financial peace and freedom for our family."

to success demands writing down your plan before you begin. When it comes to personal finance, that written intentionality takes the form of a budget.

I know, I know. No one likes to hear this notorious *b* word. I credit it to an American spirit of "'No one is going to tell me what to do with my money. *Even me!*' #merica." Perhaps that's what makes us immediately push back whenever someone suggests we budget our financial resources.

Yet here's the truth: until you shift your lens on budgeting, you'll never find true success or freedom in your finances or dig your way out of debt. Maybe it would help to recognize that a budget doesn't act as your boss. A budget isn't a school-yard bully who steals your pocket change and tortures you with a financial wedgie. A budget isn't there to make your life miserable, take away your freedom, or even stop you from spending. In fact, its purpose is quite the opposite.

> Until you shift your lens on budgeting, you'll never find true success or freedom in your finances or dig your way out of debt.

Budgets are butterflies. It's girly, I know, but stay with me here.

Budgets give you wings to fly. Budgets put stops in place to keep you from making purchases you'll later regret. Budgets let you exhale at the register total, knowing you have enough in your checking account to cover the expense. Budgets are *not* fingers tightly squeezed around your neck; they actually give you room to breathe. Budgets are not handcuffs. Budgets are the key. Budgets are not the chains that bind you. Budgets are chain breakers.

Oh, dear Money-Saving Lords and Ladies, how long it took for me to learn that a budget was not going to take away my happiness. It was there to help me enjoy true fun, and even better, *true* freedom.

The fact that a budget can be as light and delicate as a butterfly and yet as heavy and sharp as a battle-ax is one of the mysteries of the universe. A budget is certainly your most effective debt-slaying tool. With your budget, you can chop away at debt while also shielding the dollars you earn from being swallowed up by a black hole every month.

But what if you have never budgeted before? What if you have absolutely no idea where to begin? Or what if you have tried to budget repeatedly, only to come up with a big, fat fail every single time? I'm oh-so-glad you asked.

If you've never budgeted before, it is *extremely* awkward. Imagine trying to waltz without a single dance lesson . . . with a walrus . . . while wearing roller skates. Yep, that awkward. If you're married, even talking about finances may seem like a new and threatening endeavor for you and your spouse. I once instructed a large group of women to have their first budget meeting with their husbands completely naked, just to take off that awkward edge.[1] If you already feel emotionally and financially stripped bare, you might as well be physically stripped bare too. Plus, it's really hard to fight with your spouse when you're naked. (Ahem, not that I've tried.)

I digress. If you haven't the foggiest clue about how to budget or even how much you are spending per month, I suggest you begin by analyzing your finances. If you are already a budgeting pro, this is not an excuse to flip blindly through these pages or take a nap. You might be surprised to pick up a new strategy or two to add to your already rockin' budget ninja skills.

Four Basic Beginning Steps of Budgeting

1. **Write down exactly how much money you earn each month.** Whether your income is regular or sporadic, you should be able to make a good "guesstimate" of how much money you

bring in and when it typically arrives. Use old pay stubs and even last year's tax returns as you begin to chart how much you earn. If you have irregular income, don't immediately freak out when you build your budget and it redlines. Freak-outs are never helpful. Instead, take a few cleansing breaths and realize that if you are intentional, those redlines will disappear. Knowing when you will have a shortfall will help you reel in your spending and keep you from going further under.

2. **Collect your receipts and bills for a thirty- to sixty-day time frame.** Keep a record of every single penny you spend for at least a month. If you don't currently use an online app or budgeting software to monitor your spending, at the end of each day simply deposit your family's bills and receipts in a manila envelope or a basket on top of the refrigerator. Then, after your agreed-upon window of time, evaluate those receipts together.

3. **As you're tracking, it's important that you spend like you normally do.** Don't fall into one of two traps during this exercise:

    a) Try to become Ebenezer Scrooge, ratcheting down every category of expense because "we're going to be on budget if it kills us." Your outcome will be skewed, and you'll end up setting your budget at an unattainably low level that you will never be able to live within again.

    b) Spend like a Real Housewife (of any city) because you are afraid you'll never have enough money in your shoe budget. You will once again end up with an unrealistic expectation, where you budget way more than necessary for unnecessary items.

4. **Evaluate and then hatch a plan.** Once you've determined the influx and outflow of money in your household, you can begin to streamline your expenses. In what areas can you cut back? When are your bills due each month? How does this influence your budget? Can you call any of the companies to change those due dates to provide financial breathing space? This vital step determines your direction in slaying the debt dragon.

Here's a royal tip for success: Schedule a time specifically for meeting to discuss the bills and receipts when this exercise begins. Make sure you have no other commitments and power down all electronics. Come to this meeting with an open heart, prepared to learn where you spend. If you are gunning for your spouse to be the loser and you to be the winner at spending (or lack thereof), you both will be losers. Also, laying your hands palm up on the table will help you let go of your anxiety. I know, it sounds weird. But try it.

What Tools Should You Use to Budget?

The sorts of tools you use to budget will depend on your natural gifts and accessibility. By the way, this doesn't mean that those who claim that budgeting falls outside their natural gifts have an excuse not to budget. Everyone must plan how they will spend the dollars they bring into their household each month. Not having a plan is still a plan. Not budgeting is a plan to simply throw your hard-earned dollars up in the air, hoping for the best. If your debt dragons are to be slain, you *must* budget. It's simply not an optional part of your debt-slaying journey.

Some people prefer using the traditional pencil-and-paper

> Not budgeting is a plan to simply throw your hard-earned dollars up in the air, hoping for the best.

method. Others are more comfortable with technology and use software or online apps. The key is to find a method that works and that you understand—even enjoy using—so you're not discouraged and tempted to quit the process before you've barely begun. Most important, if a budgeting method has failed for you in the past, it is highly unlikely to work again, and you need to consider a new path. I love Proverbs 26:11: "As a dog eats its own vomit, so fools recycle silliness." That wording may have a high icky factor, but it's a visual metaphor hammering home the point that it's ridiculous to continue a failed method of budgeting. Don't return to a pencil-and-paper method if you constantly forget to log your expenses or are bad at math. Don't attempt using an online app or computer software if you are technologically challenged. Set yourself up for success by choosing a budgeting method that fits your family's distinct personality, lifestyle, and gifts.

I begin each morning by sitting down with a strong cup of coffee as I reconcile the prior day's expenses and glance over what bills will be due soon.[2] Brian and I have always used a software program like Quicken to forecast our income and expenses. (Isn't *forecast* a much nicer word than *budget*?) If you're a traditionalist, there's a free, simple but well-thought-out budget form printable on my website, as well as a money expenditure log. Print it out, sharpen your pencil, and begin.

How Far Out Should You Budget?

If you have never budgeted before, take small steps in this process. Don't try to make a five-year plan or even a one-year budget on your first attempt. Instead, get a month's worth of income and expenses down on paper. It may feel awkward and perhaps scary at first. Don't quit if your budget redlines because you are spending more than you are making. Quitting won't solve your debt problem. Facing the facts head-on might just help, though. Be brave, Money-Saving Lords and Ladies. You *can* do this.

Once you have developed a knack for budgeting one month at a time, begin to look at your budget through a quarterly or even biannual lens. When you do this, you'll begin to spot irregular expenses like insurance payments that aren't billed on a monthly basis, seasonal expenses like back-to-school purchases, birthdays, and one of the biggest budget busters of all, the holidays. I am most comfortable budgeting six months at a time. Doing so doesn't feel as overwhelming as trying to chart out the entire year, but it still helps me plan for events and expenses that don't occur every month.

It can be difficult to remember exactly what you spent last year on back-to-school expenses or Christmas, especially if you haven't kept solid records. Think about digging through your old bank statements if you have them. Most bank websites archive statements for months and often years at a time, so you can easily print them out even if the paper copies are long gone. If you can't come up with much data, determine to keep better records *this year* so that next year's budget will be accurate and you will not be caught off guard.

No matter how often you undertake budgeting, you *must* have regular household meetings about your family's finances. Constant communication about the flow of money in and out of our bank account was the key component of paying off $127K. At first we met at least weekly to look over when we anticipated income, as well as what bills needed to be paid and when. A couple of years into our debt-slaying journey, the King of Free took on two extra jobs, which resulted in irregular income. Each time this income arrived, we sat down as soon as it cleared to determine where that money should be spent. Typically it went directly toward our debt-repayment plan, but sometimes it was allocated for unexpected household or medical expenses. The more we communicated about our finances, the more naturally those conversations came up outside of our regularly

FIVE WAYS TO IMPROVE YOUR WEEKLY BUDGET MEETING

1. **Eliminate distractions.** Kids, electronics, phones, pets, social media, and looming deadlines all have one thing in common when it comes to your money: they seem intent on destroying your ability to accurately budget. Be sure that when you and your spouse sit down to budget, you create an environment geared for success. Make sure you haven't planned your meeting during a big game or a heavy homework night. See that the kids and pets are sleeping or otherwise occupied, and power down all your devices. If you are fighting the temptation to glance at your news feed or see which reality-show contestant has been eliminated in dramatic fashion, you will lose your focus and accomplish little. Your success (or lack thereof) is guaranteed only when distractions have been eliminated.

2. **Share a snack.** Life is better lived with something delicious to nosh on together. This doesn't mean heading to a fine-dining establishment or ordering a pizza. Keep it simple. We love stovetop popcorn. You might dish up ice cream. Sharing a snack is a simple transitional activity that allows you to escape the worries of the day, ease awkwardness, and dive into a deeper discussion. Plus, it's never a good idea to make major financial decisions when you are hungry.

3. **Come prepared.** Vague generalities and accusations destroy financial harmony. You'll find more success if you dream big together but also have an action plan with concrete facts and figures. Whether it's a stack of receipts, online research, or charts and graphs, bring those items to your budget meeting to clarify your goals. What exactly is your debt-slaying goal? What are the totals you are

seeking to eliminate? Do you want to go on a fabulous vacation next year? Exactly how much will it cost? Looking to purchase a new car or household appliance? Which model, what year, and where's the best place to buy it? Make a plan, but be flexible enough to let go of it if the two of you disagree. Coming prepared does not mean bringing a list of grievances in an attempt to overwhelm or beat down your spouse. Focus on your own behaviors and goals, not on trying to change the heart and habits of your best guy or gal.

4. Be teachable. This is perhaps the most challenging of all methods to improve your budget meetings. Deep within us dwells the desire to be right every single time. But the truth is, none of us is *always* right about everything. When you can begin to see budget meetings as a cooperative process in which you can *both* win with money rather than as an opportunity for you to prove your point or get your way, you'll truly begin to experience harmony both in your finances and in marriage. Before the meeting begins, ask yourself, *What could I learn tonight? Where do I need to change?* Allow those two simple questions to guide your heart and hands, and you are bound for budget success.

5. Dream big together. One of the biggest temptations you'll struggle with during a budget meeting is to nitpick each other over unnecessary expenses or poor choices. Avoid this temptation like the plague. Instead, dream big together. Ask the question, "What would we do with $___ a month if it were not being used for a car payment?" or "How could we make a difference in the world if we weren't saddled with debt?" Certainly, you have the hard, cold task of making sure you spend only what you make. But that doesn't mean you can't look beyond your current circumstances to catch a glimpse of what could be.

scheduled budget meeting too. Before we knew it, money was no longer a divisive area of our marriage but one that unified us instead.

What Categories Should You Include in Your Budget?

Oh, how I wish I could give you a boilerplate list of how much you should spend in every area of your life. But the categorization of expenses and amounts in each category of a budget will look different for each family. So much depends on where you live, the number of individuals in your household, your income, how much you currently owe to whom, and a litany of other wild and crazy variables. What I *can* give you is a basic list of categories that you shouldn't forget to budget for on a monthly basis. Again, it might look a little different for your family, but this is certainly a framework to build upon. I have ranked the following categories of expense in the order of need so you can determine if there are areas to cut or keep, depending on how much money is left.

> No matter how often you undertake budgeting, you *must* have regular household meetings about your family's finances.

- ○ tithing or giving[3]
- ○ rent or mortgage
- ○ food
- ○ basic personal care and household expenses (please don't give up deodorant)
- ○ utilities: electricity, gas, water, trash/sewage, and basic phone
- ○ gasoline or fuel for your vehicles
- ○ auto and home or rental insurance

○ health insurance
○ life insurance (term policy)
○ prescriptions
○ clothing (primarily for your kids; more than likely, you don't need new clothes while paying off debt)
○ car payment (after you are debt-free, this disappears and you save to pay cash for cars)
○ other loans or mortgages
○ credit card debt
○ student loan debt
○ department store credit cards
○ medical debt
○ medical expenses
○ schooling expenses
○ kids' activities
○ cell phones/smartphones
○ entertainment
○ dining out
○ cable

Once we became debt-free, all of the debt repayment categories disappeared from our budget, and we added other areas like:

○ retirement
○ a "generous" budget for the express purpose of blessing others
○ college funds for the kids
○ new car fund, also used for car maintenance[4]
○ health savings fund
○ vacation
○ Christmas

○ family gift fund for birthdays, anniversaries, and random blessings

Using a Zero-Based Budget

While we were paying off debt, Brian and I began using this strategy.[5] Essentially, a zero-based budget simply means that your goal is to "spend" each penny you bring in every month. This might mean intentionally removing extra funds from your checking account and placing them in envelopes—either physical ones or other accounts at your bank—to make sure that at the end of the month, every single penny is spent or saved. Why is this such a big deal?

Here's the thing: It's not enough to save money at the grocery store with coupons. It's not enough to save scads of coin by making your own laundry detergent. It's not enough to circle in red the amount you saved through your killer bargain hunting, often shown at the bottom of your receipt. It's not even enough to come in under budget for fun categories of spending like dining out or entertainment. You see, if

> If you leave any extra cash in your checking account at all, I promise you it will grow legs and walk to Target.

you leave any extra cash in your checking account at all, I promise you it will grow legs and walk to Target. You *must* do something with the money you save. Give it a purpose—whether that is paying off debt or saving for a fabulous vacation is up to you. Without a purpose, money will vanish and you will be unable to give an account for what you even purchased. This is why the zero-based budget strategy is essential.

Just like paying off debt, this strategy is far from complex, but it's not always easy. For those of us who are control freaks, having a zero or even a redline at the end of the month is *terrifying*. We like a little cushion in the budget, just to be sure that we don't inadvertently over-spend or—heavens to Betsy!—bounce a check. If you resonate with that, I completely commiserate. That's why I think building a small cushion of twenty-five to fifty dollars in your checking account is okay. However, don't be surprised when you overindulge just a bit and that amount disappears without your knowing where it really went.

Creating a Sporadic Income "Hit List"

If you are blessed with a monetary gift, bonus, or unexpected irregular income, you need to create a "hit list" for it. This simply means that you have a plan for such funds so they don't disappear into thin air. Whether it all goes toward debt repayment or you use it for necessary expenses beyond your regular budget, you need a plan. Be careful to use the sporadic income on items that really matter—say, to purchase a new refrigerator because yours is about to explode rather than to pick up new throw pillows because your current ones are *so* last season. While you never want to "count on" money that isn't in your hands, this hit list will allow you to have a plan for funds that arrive unexpectedly. As I mentioned, we had a combination of known and unknown income while paying off debt. We still do, which is why having a hit list is so crucial.

Perhaps *all* of your income is sporadic in nature. In that case, your hit list is your budget. You spend funds in the categories by order of importance. Having a sporadic income can make budgeting more challenging, but it is not impossible. Put away those "but we can't do that because we don't know what we are going to make next month" excuses. Your expenses don't change even if your income does. You must know how much you are spending and make a plan to live within your limits even if you can't produce a statement with income amounts.

What about Cash-Based Budgeting and All Those Envelopes?

Raise your hand if you've ever made an impulse buy. From candy bars to clearance clothes, I'm tempted every time I hit the grocery store to purchase an item (or five) that isn't on my list. As I mentioned before, I have this uncanny ability to find ridiculously awesome deals. It can be wielded for the forces of good when I'm helping someone else with their special purchases in stores or on the web. (I'm an online ninja. It's ridiculous. What are you looking for right now? Maybe I can help.) Such deals were more difficult for me to pass up before we began using a cash-based budgeting system. After all, I wasn't spending that much more than I had planned on, right?

When I use my debit card rather than cash at the grocery store, I'm much more likely to place extra items in my cart, whether they're on my list or not. I don't feel the need to keep an accurate running total of my purchases in my head. Though I'm never grossly over budget, pulling out the plastic inevitably means I don't keep my spending reined in as tightly as I should, locking in on the absolute bottom dollar.

So what's the big deal of going five or fifteen dollars over budget if you have the funds to cover it? Sure, you won't overdraw your account. Sure, it's not that much money. Sure, we've all made an impulse purchase now and then. But there's no escaping this reality: overspending with your debit card will keep you from achieving other dreams and goals.

That's why a cash envelope system can play the role of good cop when you're shopping. By putting the cash you've budgeted for household expenses like groceries and clothing in envelopes, you will be much less tempted to spring for impulse purchases that will divert funds from priorities.

The cash envelope system has been around for a *very* long time. Some sources suggest it gained popularity during the Great

Depression. In any event, buying items with cash only is not a recent phenomenon. Keep in mind that general-purpose credit cards didn't gain popularity until the 1960s.

In our world of comfort and ease, almost all of us reach in our wallets to grab the credit or debit card for our purchases. The idea of actually going to the ATM to withdraw cash or, worse yet, going into the bank to speak to a bank teller while cashing a check? *Groan.* Ain't nobody got time for that, right? *Wrong.* Paying with cash saves you more money than any coupon ever will. You spend more money when you use plastic—even if it's a debit card—rather than cash, nearly every single time.[6]

But as with any new habit, you have to be intentional about starting a cash-based budgeting system if you want it to stick. Here are a few pointers that may help:

Find an attractive envelope system. Yes, envelope systems should be practical. Don't try recycling the oversized envelope from that magazine offer. You don't want to have to fold your cash or struggle to put bills in or take them out. In addition, I have found that I fare much better with envelopes that I find inspiring or pleasant in appearance. On my site, QueenofFree.net, you can find a set of Printable Cash Envelopes with an envelope for every standard spending category. For inspiration, a different challenging but inspiring quotation is included on the back of each envelope. I designed them to be bright and cheery; in fact, they are red and yellow to match my kitchen so they look attractive hanging on the wall. I also love a company called Thrifty Zippers, which offers attractive wallets for men and women, with divisions for all of your budget categories.[7]

Ease into the process. If you are not ready to go plastic-less in every category just quite yet, I encourage you to spend only cash at the grocery store. Once you see what a difference it makes, I suspect you'll want to expand your cash experiment to dining out, entertainment, clothing, gifts, and vacations, too. Before you know it, you'll be a currency champion gymnast, sticking the landing and scoring a perfect 10 every time, with exact change to boot.

Use online bill pay or checks when it makes more sense to do so. My guess is that your electric company would begin to question your sanity if you sent them a big, fat envelope of dollar bills each month. Setting up automatic withdrawals or paying via the Internet sometimes has its place. And yes, the debit card is oh-so-handy at the gas pump (especially when you have little ones in their car seats). I use my debit card for booking hotels and flights, too. Obviously, using a debit card is not a major violation of the cash system, but you should handle it with care. Make sure to enter exact amounts into your budget log within twenty-four hours of purchase so that you don't forget how much you have spent.

Budgeting Is a Marathon, Not a Sprint

You will find that you gain skill in budgeting the more you do it. Just like learning to ride a bike or play a musical instrument, the longer you practice budgeting, the greater success you will gain.

Even so, I am certain you will slip up in the budgeting process sometimes. Here's my vulnerable moment: even though we paid off all of that debt, we still sometimes fail to plan for an expense. *School yearbooks get me every single year.* You will sometimes underestimate the amount you need to spend. Your sump pump will run all night long, and the electric bill will be ridiculously high (yep, that happened last month). It's okay. Adjust your spending. Cut back. Look for a temporary job. Sell something you own. Then get back on the budgeting horse and try again. Not having a plan will get you nowhere fast. Doing something is always better than doing nothing, even if you fall short.

Budgeting is also a great reminder that everything you've been given is a gift from God. That includes

your spouse
your children
your income
your talents
your job
your home
your odd assortment of canned goods

These are all valuable treasures He's entrusted to your safe care. In Proverbs 21:20, King Solomon offers a wise perspective on the role of budgeting in your life: "Valuables are safe in a wise person's home; fools put it all out for yard sales." Budgeting is the contemplative practice of guaranteeing we aren't placing these blessings in yard sales. A budget helps us track the valuables (our income) God has blessed us with and keeps us from making rash purchases or spending more than we make. When we don't track how much money is entering and exiting our home, in a sense we are playing the role of the fool, metaphorically putting our valuables out in the front yard, on sale for one hundredth of what they're actually worth.

Your enemy is debt, not the budget.

Your enemy is debt, not the budget. Sure, a budget might look big and scary at the onset of your journey. But I promise that after you slay your debt dragon, your budget will be the trusty sidekick every warrior needs. Frodo needed Samwise. Batman had Robin. The Lone Ranger relied on Tonto. You *need* your budget. Stop seeing this tool as an adversary. Begin to look at it as your essential, long-term battle companion.

Debt-Slaying Strategies

✓ Write down exactly how much money you earn as a household per month. Don't forget to include both known income and estimated sporadic income based on prior months or years. You'll also want to record revenues received through child support, dividends, or stipends.

✓ If you've never set budget category amounts before, commit to collecting your receipts for the next thirty to sixty days to get a good idea of where you should set your limits. Go and find a basket or an envelope right now. Decorate it or just leave it plain, but place it in a common area of your house where you'll remember to deposit receipts daily.

✓ Schedule a budget meeting with your spouse (or a trusted friend) for next week. Don't forget to implement the strategies to improve communication listed in this chapter.

✓ Choose at least one category of spending (I vote for the grocery store!) in which to use only cash for a month. See if it makes a difference.

Chapter 5

AT THE ROYAL TABLE

Hey there! All who are thirsty, come to the water! Are you penniless? Come
anyway—buy and eat! Come, buy your drinks, buy wine and milk. Buy without
money—everything's free! Why do you spend your money on junk food, your
hard-earned cash on cotton candy? Listen to me, listen well: Eat only the best, fill
yourself with only the finest. Pay attention, come close now, listen carefully to my
life-giving, life-nourishing words. I'm making a lasting covenant commitment
with you, the same that I made with David: sure, solid, enduring love.

ISAIAH 55:1-5

TRUE CONFESSION: despite careful budgeting, I make more mistakes with
my money when it comes to food than I do in any other category
of spending. I make impulse buys in the grocery store. I have been
known to take harried trips through the drive-through. My kids have
asked the age-old question "What's for dinner tonight?" only to hear
me say, "Um, I don't know" more times than I'd like to remember.
Fortunately, over the past several years I've learned some key strategies
for planning meals, shopping for groceries, and dining out that have
helped my family eat healthfully while slaying debt.

Interestingly, more people ask me about how to save on food
purchases and packing lunches than about any other area of their

finances. Most budget-conscious people mean well. They want to feed their families nutritious meals. They want to stay on budget. They want to eat at home on a regular basis, pack leftovers, and have healthy but affordable snacks available to their kids after school. But let's face it, sometimes life gets in the way.

Back in 2008, when the King of Free and I began to evaluate our finances and spending habits, I was terrified to get a handle on just how much we were spending on eating out. I knew a larger-than-necessary percentage of our income was financing the dining establishments near our house. Our then five-year-old Princess Eldest knew nearly every restaurant logo in the greater Midwest. Four years later, I was able to see the sharp contrast with her sister, the Princess Youngest, who referred to Chick-fil-A as "chicken" and Fazoli's as "spaghetti's" until she was well over the age of four. These were the only two restaurants she knew, and she dined at them so rarely that she didn't even know their correct names. However, she could pick out the ALDI, Meijer, and Target logos and knew coupon lingo. She could also identify Dave Ramsey by picture, voice, and printed name at the age of two. Children reflect our patterns in life, don't they?

We *all* have to eat on a regular basis. In fact, I love to do so. Food is one of my favorite things about living. You *should* be budgeting plenty to provide for your family's nutritional needs, as well as the grand enjoyment that is eating. What a blessing God has given us in the form of our taste buds! He allows us to literally feast on a daily basis. As with every other area of our lives, though, He calls us to be good stewards of these blessings. From eating nutritionally dense foods that keep you fuller for longer periods of time to keeping enough ingredients on hand to throw together five to seven meals *without* grocery shopping, waging a heated battle against the debt dragon often begins in the kitchen.

Meal Planning

Before you even step into a grocery store, you can begin the attack on the debt dragon in your kitchen simply by following two cardinal rules.

Plan ahead. While not a self-help book or leadership manual, the Bible has plenty to say about time management. Check out this verse from Proverbs: "Careful planning puts you ahead in the long run; hurry and scurry puts you further behind" (21:5). Hurry and scurry? I have lived these words again and again because I failed to plan. Slaying the debt dragon caused me to dump old habits and bring more intentionality to my time.

On the side of my refrigerator hangs a meal planning form I created called "On the Royal Table This Week." I update it every week and see it daily as I come and go. My meal planner (which, by the way, you can print for free from QueenofFree.net) is a stabilizing force in my busy world as a working mom. Just as with a budget, I learned to look at planning meals as a liberating force in my life rather than a restrictive weapon to squelch my creativity. I began jotting down my meal plans every week early in our debt-slaying journey. Now I share my plan every Monday on my website. It's not an invitation to come to my house for dinner (wouldn't that be amazingly fun!); however, it might spark a few ideas for a plan of your own.

I'll tell you more about the basics of creating meal plans later in this chapter, as well as how a little preparation in creating grocery lists and organizing coupons can save you both time and frustration.

Begin with what you have. I love reading about the miracle God performed through Elisha for a destitute widow (see 2 Kings 4:1-7). She came to Elisha when her children were about to be sold into

THE QUEEN OF FREE'S PANTRY TOP TEN

These ten items guarantee our family could quickly throw together a meal at any point in time. We try to always keep them in the pantry and fridge to keep ourselves out of the drive-through.

1. Peanut butter
2. Bread
3. Fresh-cut veggies (peppers, onions, mushrooms, carrots, spinach)
4. Eggs
5. Cheese
6. Rice
7. Tomato paste or spaghetti sauce
8. Olive oil
9. Pasta
10. Applesauce

WHAT'S YOUR PANTRY TOP TEN?

1.
2.
3.
4.
5.
6.
7.
8.
9.
10.

slavery because of her debt (now that is *real* debt; what you are facing is nothing in comparison). Elisha asked her how he could help and what she had in her home. Her response? "*Nothing,*" she said. "Well, I do have a little oil."[1]

In the Queen of Free Translation (QoFT), I hear the widow stretching out the word *well.* Money-Saving Lords and Ladies, can I just be honest for a brief moment? So many times I have minimized the gifts God has given me with a "wellllllllll" of my own.

"Wellllllllll, we don't make that much money, so we don't have that much to give."

"Wellllllllll, I'm only a stay-at-home mom; what kind of calling could God have for my life?"

"Wellllllllll, our home is so small, we couldn't open it up to anyone on a regular basis."

Moral of the story: take care to use your *wellllllllll* well.

But oh, how I can relate to this woman when it comes to feeling like there's nothing in the cabinets! "There is *nothing* to eat in this *entire* house." How many times have those very untrue words rolled across my tongue? If you live in America, the odds of you having nothing to eat in your home are little to none. I'm sure you almost always have *some-thing*—even if it is merely "a little oil."

When drawing up your food battle plans against the debt dragon, begin with what you have. Open your fridge, your freezer, your cabinets, and your pantry and ask yourself, *If I had to make a meal right now without purchasing anything, what would I fix?* More than likely, you could eke out one or maybe even two meals with items you currently have without spending a dime. Granted, you might create some odd concoctions, but merely looking through the lens of

> Merely looking through the lens of plenty rather than dearth sparks both gratitude and creativity when it comes to food.

plenty rather than dearth sparks both gratitude and creativity when it comes to food.

After you plan a meal or two based on what you already have in your home, begin to think about what single ingredients you could add to make additional meals, so you can cut down on your purchases at the grocery store. For example, perhaps you have both pasta and sauce but need to buy a protein source to accompany the dish. Or you have everything for your world-famous homemade pizza, except cheese. Add those missing ingredients to your grocery list and the meals to your plan. God might be able to work an everyday miracle with that little bit of oil you already have.

That was certainly the case for the widow. Elisha instructed her to gather as many containers as she could. Can't you just imagine her two sons running up and down the streets, asking everyone they knew for more pots, pitchers, and vats? Their friends, family, and neighbors must have thought them a little bit crazy too, right?

After they had amassed their many vessels, this little family was to close and lock the door behind them. The miracle God was getting ready to do in their midst was for their eyes only. Sometimes God puts on a dazzling display for everyone to see. Sometimes His power is meant for a personal witness. Who knows, maybe He plans on doing a little of both during your debt-slaying journey.

The widow began measuring out her "welllllllll, a little oil" into each container, pouring until it was filled to the top. Her sons continued handing her empty jug after empty jug. Imagine her shock when she asked for the next empty jug, only to realize every one of them was filled! The oil didn't continue pouring onto the floor. It stopped. The family had what they needed.

Elisha told the woman to sell the oil to settle her debts and then live, along with her sons, on what remained. God's blessing was enough. The widow didn't start an oil boutique. She didn't charge admission to a miracle oil-multiplying show. God didn't flood her home with oil until she and her sons were doing the backstroke in thick liquid. He gave them what they needed.

God provides for my family too. He has done unbelievable miracles in our lives. Our household survives and even thrives. Time and time again, my "welllllllll, a little oil" is multiplied in miraculous form. Yet somehow I miss the amazing marvel God has performed in my life. I'm not satisfied the way I should be, resting in His provision, confident in His record of always showing up. I forget to share His blessing with others, hoarding the miracle all to myself. I'm not sure what it says about the condition of my soul that I always long for more than what is needed. How much better off my heart would be if I paused and realized over and over again how many times God has provided just enough.

Count on God to provide what you need. Fight the temptation to want more. Most of all, don't forget to give God the glory in the midst of your "welllllllll." Maybe we would all be a little better off if we recorded the journey, sharing the ups, downs, and especially the moments of provision that leave us with our mouths gaping and our hearts fluttering. God wants to tell a story, even through our "welllllllll" moments in meal planning.

Four meal-planning "musts"

So I hear you. You're not a Rachael Ray and can only dream about living the life of the Pioneer Woman (isn't she lovely?). You don't have to be a gourmet chef or even a foodie blogger to create meal plans; you simply need to be willing to invest a bit of time and planning into the process. Being proactive at the beginning of the week will mean no mad dashes to the grocery store or drive-through later on—which will save you both money and time in the long run.

These four keys have guided my meal planning for six years. Each week, I ask myself the same questions all over again to guide the process and keep our family on track.

Ask the right questions. As I mentioned in the previous section, it's important to begin by considering what you have when making your meal plan. Some good questions to consider at the start are:

What meals could I prepare *without* a trip to the grocery store?
What recipe ingredients (e.g., sour cream, meats, vegetables) are about to expire or go bad?

It's also important to consider your family's schedule for the coming week.

Which nights of the week will require a quick and easy plan?
Which nights could I spend more time cooking and preparing elements for meals later in the week?

Once you have considered those details, it's time to plan out the main dishes and side dishes for your dinners. That boils down to a final question:

What specifically will we be eating each evening?

Survey your family and ask them which dishes are their favorites. Are they okay with eating breakfast for dinner? Obviously no one gets a pass on eating nutritiously. Fruits and veggies aren't optional. However, the input you receive from your spouse and/or kids might surprise you and help guide your thinking.

We often fall into patterns of eating the same dishes on the same nights of the week—Taco Tuesday! Pizza Friday! As much as I thought that everyone would become bored with the regular schedule, they really don't seem to mind. Plus, I find great ways to vary those recurring meals.

SURVEY SAYS! QUESTIONS TO ASK YOUR FAMILY ABOUT FOOD

While there are plenty of great resources to help you plan meals, none is as valuable as your own family. Their answers to the following questions will make meal planning much easier and more realistic. This simple survey might also spark other questions you want to ask your spouse and kids.

1. My favorite meal we eat at home is _____ .

2. If I had to eat the same thing every night, it would be _____ .

3. My favorite vegetable is _____ .

4. Breakfast for dinner is
        a. weird!
        b. delicious.
        c. okay every once in a while.

5. My favorite fruit is _____ .

6. The best meal I ever had was _____ .

7. (For adults only) I won't eat _____ .

8. Other favorites or ideas: _____

Write it down. You may already be weary of my haranguing to write down your plans for life. *If you don't put words on paper, every area of your life will just happen to you, instead of being under your intentional watch.* Meal planning is no different from budgeting. Good intentions will get you nowhere fast. You must physically write down your plan. You can use good ole pencil and paper like I do, or find an app or online service. There are wonderful websites that offer meal planning services for a fee. (Of course, I am too cheap to actually pay for anything in this life. I am the Queen of Free, not the Queen of Spending Money, after all.) However, if coming up with menu ideas and building grocery lists is such a challenge that you will be paralyzed and do nothing at all, you should investigate sites like eMeals or Food on the Table. You can take to Pinterest to get ideas too. I'm a bit of a Pinterest junkie, but if you've never used this social media site, think of it as a clearinghouse of recipes, life hacks, and so much more. It's as simple as signing up for a free account and then searching "meal plan." Thousands of resources will suddenly be available to you.

> If you don't put words on paper, every area of your life will just happen to you, instead of being under your intentional watch.

Just don't get sucked into an endless black hole of options. Again, you would fare much better asking your family for their favorites and then building a plan based on their collective preferences than you would spending four hours online researching recipes. Trying to become a fine dining chef in your "spare" time is unlikely to aid you in your journey to slaying your debt dragon. Keep it simple, Money-Saving Lords and Ladies.

Follow the seasons. Consider what items are on sale and in season when building a meal plan. Where I live, buying blueberries in

December will stretch our family's grocery budget beyond recognition. Grocery store circulars, available either in print or online, will let you know which items are a good fit for your weekly meal plan and which items you will have to wait a few months to enjoy. Again, practice makes perfect. The more you plan meals, the more skilled you will become in recognizing seasonal sales at the grocery store.

Schedule dining out. My least favorite guessing game goes like this:

> "Where do you want to go for dinner?"
> "I dunno. What do you want?"

Don't tell me you haven't played it before too. We dined out very rarely while paying off debt, and the King of Free spent two and a half years of our four-year journey without eating at a single restaurant (more on that later), but when we did, it was a scheduled event on the meal plan. We even preselected where we would be eating. It became a blessing—"Yay! We are going out to eat at (insert favorite restaurant here)!"—rather than a curse:

> "What sounds good?"
> "Nothing."
> "What about _____?"
> "I don't like that place. What about the new Mexican place?"
> "We had tacos yesterday."

Please tell me someone else has these insane conversations too! Bottom line: if you have budgeted to dine out, then include that in your meal plan. You will actually look forward to the experience rather than settling for a just so-so meal or dinner at the closest restaurant to your home. Dining out should be looked forward to as a gift, not dreaded as drudgery.

The Battle of the Grocery Store Aisles

I have a love-hate relationship with grocery shopping. I can wield a coupon quicker than a ninja throws a star. I know that grocery shopping will result in my family making healthier decisions. I know that grocery shopping is oh-so-much better than eating out for both our budget and our behinds. However, I'd much rather stay in my pajamas all day than cruise the aisles with the one cart that has the wonky wheel (which I seem to find every time I shop!). I can rock a sale, save 57 percent off my bill, and still dread the entire experience. In fact, I'm getting tired just typing these words. Grocery stores wear me out.

One trip in particular was so draining that I still remember it with a shudder—even ten years later. Several weeks before Christmas, I went to Walmart where, in addition to my usual grocery shopping, I picked up holiday baking items, decorations, cards, and more.

I piled my cart high without estimating the total very well. And I waited in a long line to check out. As the cashier rang up my final items, my heart skipped a beat. The total was well over $200. Even in my wild spending days, this was not a number I often reached unless there were big ticket items in the cart (which there weren't).

I had nickeled-and-dimed my way to over $200 of holiday "things," most of which we did not need. I wanted to cry as I dug in my purse for my wallet. And then it happened.

I didn't have my wallet.

A wave of relief rushed over me. I couldn't pay for these items. Literally. Embarrassed, I told the cashier that I had left my wallet in the car and said I would be back. I placed the cart at customer service. But when I got to the car, I realized my wallet wasn't there either. I had left it at home. I drove there to get it but then decided not to go back.

A bit of distance helped me realize we didn't need most of those items. Too embarrassed to return to the same store, I went to another retailer later in the day and spent much less, getting only what we needed.[2]

You see why I have a grocery store aversion? After just a couple of experiences where I had to pick my jaw up off the ground at the checkout, I knew I needed accountability and a plan. While we were paying off $127K in debt, I learned to place some intentional stops in my life to prevent overspending at the grocery store. I like to call these rules my "Grocery Store Ten Commandments."

Nobody likes rules. We feel that they stifle our creativity. We think they want to take away our joy. But the truth is, *rules are guidelines that keep our lives in check.* They help our children remember to brush their teeth. They keep people from barreling down the highway at breakneck speed. If applied wisely, they can also keep us from overspending. I know that my "Grocery Store Ten Commandments" *still* help me save money on a routine basis. They are not complicated. They do not require hours of preparation. And yes, they are simply guidelines (occasionally I do break one and am *not* struck down by lightning).

1. **Thou *shalt not* shop when you are hungry.** Akin to meal planning, this commandment might seem obvious. In fact, if you want to buy a ton of junk food and bust your food budget, go to the grocery store hungry and without a plan. A prewritten battle plan will save you time, money, and the need to run three extra miles this week. Also, shopping hungry will make you angry, a state of being I like to refer to as "hangry."[3]

2. **Thou *shalt not* shop after 9 p.m.** This is also known as my "rule of the *Gremlins.*" Remember that 1980s movie with the cuddly little brown-and-white bear things that went all crazy green skinned and pointy toothed if you fed them after midnight? It could be just me, but I can get completely disoriented in a superstore after the hour of nine o'clock. I wind up

purchasing way too many breakfast foods for the next morning or wandering the aisles aimlessly for hours on end.

3. **Thou *shalt* shop the perimeter.** Healthier and more affordable foods—fresh fruit, veggies, meats, dairy, etc.—are found on the perimeter of the store. Processed, pricey junk food resides in the center aisles. Do not waste your money on food that will expand your waistline and leave you craving more fat, sugar, and calories. Go for healthy, nutritiously dense foods that will fill you up longer. At the top of my list are always fresh and frozen produce, lean meat, nuts, oats, and dairy items (everything is better with cheese on top).

4. **Thou *shalt* use cash only.** I am passionate about this commandment and find that when I follow it religiously, I stay on target with our budget and our needs. The points on your debit or credit card will not save you as much as using cash will. I find that even the most conscientious shoppers overspend by ten to fifteen dollars a week when using plastic. Spending dollars and cents keeps you from blowing your budget and creates a hedge around it.

   You will keep a closer eye on your total as you shop. When you are out of money, you are done shopping. Have an emergency? Well, certainly it is okay to use your debit card to cover it. But using cash will cause you to pause and question the true nature of such an emergency. Or you just might decide to put back another item in your cart in order to purchase what you truly need.

5. **Thou *shalt* take three to five items out of your cart before checking out.** This is my favorite shopping tip of all time. It is the simplest way to save at least five to ten dollars on each grocery store trip. It requires no coupons, and unless you are a list

commando, you probably picked up a few items you simply do not need or can wait to purchase on a more flexible week. Politely place the items back on the shelves or hand them to the cashier and say, "No, thank you." Do *not* leave them on an end cap, which will create more work for an employee. Then do a small victory dance in the checkout lane.

6. **Thou *shalt not* shop for leisure.** Trips to Target or Walmart should not be listed on your résumé under "Hobbies." If you play with snakes, you are bound to get bitten. Stay out of the store unless you need to be there.

7. **Thou *shalt* look high and look low.** The most expensive foods are placed at eye level. I'm no marketing strategist, but I understand that what you see ends up in your cart. While I have no research to back it up, I also strongly believe that the most enticing and expensive items are placed at the eye level of the average toddler. How else can you explain the need for big bouncy balls in the food aisles?

   The most economical foods will probably be difficult to find on the shelves. Stoop down or tiptoe up. Keep your eyes peeled for the best prices because they may be out of your line of sight.

8. **Thou *shalt* shop with your spouse on occasion.** Typically, the chore of grocery getting falls on the shoulders of one spouse. If this is true in your household, make sure to shop together periodically. Because I do not particularly enjoy grocery shopping, anytime I can ~~cajole~~ convince Brian to go with me, this mundane task becomes a little bit more bearable. Have I mentioned how much I enjoy spending time with my man? He can make the produce section steamy. I may have frightened him a time or two when I was able to quote prices without looking at them. Numbers just stick in my head, whether I want them

to or not.[4] Brian's trust in my judgment grows each time we go to the store together, as he observes my attention to detail and drive to get the absolute best deal possible.

Maybe it's not exactly a romantic date night filled with flowers and music (although they have both of those at our grocery store, and like I said, my man can make the freezer section melt). Still, it will be as fun as you make it. Don't shop before a meal (see Grocery Store Commandment #1), and keep the mood light. Again, this is not your opportunity to berate your spouse for overspending. Instead, it's a platform of communication to draw you closer to each other.

9. **Thou *shalt* have a written plan.** It bears repeating. Every great tactician needs a strategy. You cannot go into battle without one. Shopping without a list is just begging the store to take your retirement savings and smack you in the mouth too. My grocery list probably looks like spy code to anyone who sees it in my cart. I make notations and shorthand to help me remember how many of each item I should buy and whether or not I have coupons to correspond with the purchase. Remember that free printable meal planner on QueenofFree. net? On the sidebar, it has two columns for your grocery list so while you're planning your meals you can also note what you need. I typically shop two stores per week (ALDI and whichever big box retailer maximizes my coupons), so I use one column for each store. I *might* take list making to a whole new level of geeking when I put my items in order of where I'll find them in the store. Your written plan doesn't have to look like mine. It just needs to be legible and strategic enough for you to stay on track, without overspending.

10. **Thou *shalt* use coupons.** I will be the first to admit that I am not extreme when it comes to couponing. But did you know

YOUR GROCERY STORE TEN COMMANDMENTS

1.
2.
3.
4.
5.
6.
7.
8.
9.
10.

that the average American millionaire uses coupons?[5] I figure if I want a few extra zeros at the end of my income someday, I should probably espouse the theory. Couponing saves me an average of $35 a week, and I spend only one to two hours in total preparation. Thirty-five dollars an hour is not too shabby an hourly rate, no?

I encourage you to develop a set of commandments unique to your shopping habits and family's lifestyle. What works for me might not work for you and vice versa. Now is the time. Here is your chance. Luckily, you do not need a quill and a piece of parchment or a stone tablet and a chisel.

Simply pull out a pen and paper to compose your own sacred rules of grocery shopping.

O Coupons, Wherefore Art Thou?

I could write an entire book about how to most effectively use coupons without losing your mind. (Go ahead and make that suggestion to my publisher.) When we began our debt-slaying journey, there was no such thing as *Extreme Couponing* and the iPhone was brand-new, so digital coupons were as distant a dream as George Jetson's jet pack. The landscape of how to use coupons successfully has changed quite a bit since 2008. By the time you get to this chapter, things may have changed even more. Still, there are timeless principles to apply when couponing.

Don't spend more time couponing than you would working for a wage. If you are spending sixty hours a week clipping coupons, you might be a . . . wait, wait, that's another monologue I once heard delivered by Jeff Foxworthy. Just kidding! Ideally, couponing should take only an hour or two a week. I encourage you to develop your own strategy, one in which you spend small chunks of time clipping, organizing, and matching coupons to sales. I like to multitask for this—hunting coupons while partaking in a guilty pleasure hour of TV. Your time is worth money too. So if you find yourself bogged down in couponing and are measuring your life's worth in toilet paper, candy bars, and sticks of deodorant, you might need to consider a new game plan.

It's a good idea to keep your meal plan nearby while you're clipping. That way, you can be intentional about keeping and organizing only those coupons that you truly need and you won't be tempted by offers that do not apply. Speaking of organization, there are plenty of great methods you could employ—from divided envelopes to boxes to stacks and more. I've found the most success using a one-and-a-half-inch binder filled with the plastic sleeves that baseball card collectors use to store their cards. I place one coupon in each little slot, making sure the quantity, product description, and expiration date can all be easily read. Similar to my list-making tendencies, the pages of the binder are organized by aisles in the store.

The store where I use coupons most frequently has produce, deli, and bread items at the front. So I keep coupons for those items in the first and second pages, followed by coupons for frozen items that I find in the next two aisles. In the middle of the binder, I have individual sections for store coupons that I've printed out from home or received at the register. That way, I can easily flip to only the coupons I need for a specific store. I also keep two to three pages in the very back for store royalty cards, gift cards (they fit perfectly!), and random coupons for restaurants or service industries (dry cleaning, oil changes, entertainment). There's a pouch for oversized coupons too. Again, this is the method that works best for me. It will be important for you to find an organizational strategy that fits your unique gifts and partners well with your personality.

Just in case you're wondering, I do lug my binder with me everywhere I go. In the early days, I was caught off guard a couple of times, leaving behind a coupon that I needed or suddenly discovered paired perfectly with a sale. This always caused great wailing and gnashing of teeth for me. So forever I shall be a binder-toting girl. I have other friends who bring a small photo album (think the brag books you can purchase at a dollar store) with only the coupons they need for a specific trip. Again, your method will depend upon your preference.

Don't hoard what you score. After combining coupons and store sales, I'm sometimes able to pick up two bottles of shampoo, tubes of toothpaste, or razors for next to nothing. I am a fan of stockpiling . . . within reason. I want to be able to care for my family and even bless others with the fruits of my coupon labor. However, we live in a very small house, so keeping a year's worth of supplies on hand just isn't feasible. If you have the space, time, and energy to build a supply of things that you will truly use, by all means prep away. But if you suddenly died and your neighbors had to clean out your closets, don't shock and awe them with thousands of tubes of toothpaste. I find it valuable to keep one or two extra items or packages of a specific product on hand when I can. But you *do not* have to stockpile to pay off debt. Stocking up a great deal feels wonderful and truly is useful. However, if you are spending beyond your budget, the bottom line won't work out, and you will be left only with bottles of shampoo to comfort your sadness. Shiny hair isn't worth it, Money-Saving Lords and Ladies. Slaying the debt dragon comes first. Stockpiling always comes second.

Having a supply of extra products on hand can be a blessing when you use it to help someone else. I'll never forget the time the Princess Eldest cleared out our little assortment of shampoo and conditioner to donate it to the Red Cross when flooding forced people in our community out of their homes.

Stockpiling can also be a trap. There's an age-old temptation to trust in things more than we trust in God. We see our stuff and exhale, "We will be okay." Jesus tells the story of a man who was very good at stockpiling. In fact, he had stored up so much grain that he tore down his barns just to build bigger ones for more grain. The man suddenly died, and all of his work was for naught. Jesus ends His story with a warning: "Yes, a person is a fool to store up earthly wealth but not have a rich relationship with God" (Luke 12:21, NLT).

Don't purchase what you won't use. My basic rule of thumb is that I never make a first-time purchase just because I have a coupon. While coupons are wonderful tools in the right hands, they are still a marketing campaign in your newspaper. My Pollyanna-self wishes I could tell you that companies long to bless you by saving you fifty cents off that new! and improved! product. However, they really long for you to *buy* their new product.

One common trap I see new couponers fall into is picking up items that they won't or can't use simply because said products are free or close to free. Both your time and space are valuable. So if you don't have a dog but can get dog food for free, either (a) resist the temptation to snag the freebie or (b) have a plan in place to donate the food to a shelter or give it to a friend within twenty-four hours. If you cannot give away something within that time frame, the likelihood of it growing roots and becoming a permanent fixture in your home goes up exponentially.

Go digital. Probably one of the biggest coupon roadblocks is forgetting coupons at home. *Veni, vidi, vici.* You clipped. You strategized. You forgot. (Perhaps my Latin is a little rusty?) Enter the new era of digital coupons where you "clip" coupons online and then attach them to your phone number (it can even be a dumb phone like I long used, not a fancy-pants Android or iPhone) or a store savings card. Simply enter your number or scan your card, and your savings will be automatically deducted, without even letting the cashier know that you are using coupons. My favorites in this category include Meijer's mPerks program, Target's Cartwheel, and the coupons you can clip to your Kroger Plus card (or Kroger affiliates). After watching trends in couponing over the last five or six years, I see more coupon programs moving in this direction. Investigating digital coupons at your favorite grocery or superstore is well worth your while.

Realize that this life is a marathon, not a sprint. This truth bears repeating because there are so many categories of life where this principle applies. You will forget to purchase your Sunday newspaper. You will leave your coupons at home. You will spend more money than necessary now and then. However, this does not mean that you give up on saving money altogether. Instead, get back on the horse and try, try again. (Did I just mix a running metaphor with a jockey metaphor? Why yes, I did.) Never give up on a debt-slaying habit just because you made one little misstep. Return to couponing, and saving money shall return to you.

Dig Out Your Care Bears Lunchbox

"Brown bag, brown bag, what do you carry?"

"I carry the key to your ability to pay off debt more quickly."

Packing lunches made a huge shift in our financial world. Even school lunches are radically overpriced compared to what you can provide from your own royal rations for your princes and princesses. Eating out during the noon hour must be eliminated if you are serious about slaying the debt dragon.

The King of Free took this principle to heart, and for two-and-a-half *years*, he ate nothing from a restaurant. Not a meal, not a cup of coffee, not an ice cream cone, not even a glass of water. Even if someone else was picking up the tab, he abstained. Honestly, at first it was an act of discipline, but then it turned into a full-on "guy streak" that couldn't be broken. (You know, like the guy who won't wash his gym socks because then his team will lose?) For some reason, people longed to see Brian fail in this endeavor, or perhaps they simply marveled at his extreme intentionality.[6]

At first, co-diners thought him incredibly weird and were uncomfortable eating restaurant food while he snacked on leftovers from a brown bag. Often when Brian mentioned that he didn't dine out, he was met with the rejoinder, "Well, you can't *not* eat at restaurants." (Side note: if you want to successfully pay off debt, you have to become used to people thinking that you are weird and different. Paying off debt *is* weird in this culture. Taking the necessary steps to pay off debt is unusual and out of the norm, but that is okay. Most success in life comes from marching to the beat of a different drum. Rock it out, baby, and twirl those sticks in the air.) Eventually Brian's friends and colleagues became used to the oddity and didn't even notice it.

Restaurants are not necessary to our existence. For centuries, people lived without drive-throughs or fancy, sit-down, fine dining experiences. The human race survived (with less B-roll footage of obesity for the news to boot). Don't get me wrong, restaurants are a *blessing* and a good gift. I love a fancy coffee drink or a night when I don't have to cook and clean for everyone else. However, move the experience of dining out from the "need" category to the "want" category for financial success. It's okay to *want* to eat out on occasion. But it is *never* a need. While you are paying off debt, you must get much more familiar with the inside of your kitchen and your lunchbox.

If you do choose to budget monthly dining-out dollars for lunch or dinner, be sure that you use them in context with the cash-based envelope system. You are so much less likely to feel the expense with your debit or credit card than you are when you actually hand over George Washingtons to the waiter or waitress. Keeping a cash envelope for eating out will curb how much you order and how many times you head out to eat on the town.

Eight tips for packing a lunch

1. **What should you pack?** Obviously leftovers are the top choice for most people. I try to make enough dinner for at least one extra serving for this very purpose. During temperate weather, I marinate and then grill an entire bag of frozen chicken on Mondays. That night we have a dish that features the chicken, and then I chop the remaining breasts and store them in the fridge. It's simple to toss this great lean protein source into a salad or some pasta or make it into a sandwich. I find that I'm

at ease knowing that the chicken is always there as an option if we don't have enough leftovers. During the winter months, I purchase a small precooked ham. Look for them in the meat department rather than at the deli counter. Lower in cost than deli ham, their thick slices stretch further.

2. **Ditch the juice box.** Avoid packing juice boxes, sodas, and bottled water. This is our family's "congreenient" lunchbox strategy that saves both our money and the earth's resources. Rather than purchasing individual beverage servings, purchase a sturdy, nonleaking, reusable bottle to fill daily with your favorite drink. You'll recoup your up-front cost in about a week's time. Typically our beverage of choice is water (woo-hoo for *free*!).

   If you plan to send such a bottle with young children, make sure they can actually open and close it without assistance before you purchase it. If it's difficult to open in the aisle of the superstore, it will be difficult for them to open under time constraints at the cafeteria table when you are not there to assist.

3. **Be sure you have enough.** Don't blow your lunch-bringing strategy by packing too light. The last thing you want to do is to have a moment of weakness and pay ten times what you should on a vending machine purchase, which is almost always something you'll regret eating later too. Pack snacks like fresh-cut vegetables, whole fruits, whole grain crackers and cheese, whole raw nuts, string cheese, yogurt, or granola. Any one of these snacks will still be good later in the week if you don't eat them on the day you bring them with you.

4. **Stash PB-and-J supplies at the office.** If you can, keep jars of peanut butter and fruit spread in your break room or desk.

That way, if push comes to shove, you can grab a couple of pieces of bread on the way out the door and have a simple lunch. More than likely, you'll have a leftover snack from a day earlier in the week to pair with this childhood favorite. It's also a great idea to keep some instant oatmeal at work for those days when you skip breakfast because you are pinched for time.

5. **Skip the prepackaged, lunchbox-sized portions.** If you purchase the teeny bags of chips or even individually packaged veggies, you might gain a minute or two of extra time, but you'll be paying over double the price per ounce. With reusable containers or even plastic bags, you can easily create your own preportioned sizes and save a bundle.

6. **Step away from the chips.** As tasty as they are, chips and pretzels are not wise lunch choices. Sure, they taste great with your deli sandwich, but they are both more expensive than fruits and veggies and leave you feeling hungry only an hour later. That will lead you to eat *and* spend more in the long run. Pack high-quality nutritional foods (lean meats and cheese, whole grains, fruits, vegetables) that take longer to digest so you stay full longer and keep the munchies at bay.

7. **Spend time preparing items on Sunday evening.** It's so easy to fall into a pattern of fly-by-the-seat-of-your-pants lunchbox preparations in the morning. Been there, done that. Instead, spend the close of the weekend preparing your lunchbox items in advance. Peel, cut, and bag carrots. Pop and then divide a big batch of popcorn into smaller bags.

You can even make your own crustless PB-and-J sandwiches, using your favorite bread, nut butter, and jelly. Remove the crusts and seal the sandwiches with a handy-dandy kitchen tool. Then bag and freeze them. Your sammie sans crust will double as a cold pack and a main dish. Best of all, it will be perfectly thawed by the noon hour.

Preparing items on Sunday evenings allows your princes and princesses to put together their own lunchboxes quickly and effectively on busy mornings. Require them to drop in one protein, one fruit, one veggie, and one treat. That's a double bonus: save time and teach independence to your children. Thirty minutes on a Sunday evening will buy you more time to drink coffee and decrease the likelihood of bedhead on busy weekday mornings.

8. **Find reliable, reusable containers.** From your lunchbox to the water bottle, you want to find a bag and reusable containers that will stand the test of time. *Always* check to see if they are dishwasher safe (many less expensive options are not) and again that your children can open and close them with ease. Give any containers the once-over to check for the potential to leak as well.

The best time to shop for these items? Pick up lunchboxes and bags in the clearance aisle a month or two after all the back-to-school sales. Use a "middle of the road" theory when it comes to how much you pay for lunchboxes and food storage containers. Skip the dollar section but stay away from the high-end items, too. Cheap containers often fall apart after a few months and will need to be replaced. Stick with items that will last a year or longer.

You Can Still Feast While Your Finances Fast

Who knew eating and paying off debt were so closely linked? Consider what God says: "Why spend money on what is not bread, and your labor on what does not satisfy? Listen, listen to me, and eat what is good, and you will delight in the richest of fare" (Isaiah 55:2, NIV).

It can be overwhelming to contemplate the many ways food and finances intersect. Slaying the debt dragon doesn't require eating dust from the corner of your cabinets, choking down ramen noodles, or even existing on a daily diet of beans and rice (although we *did* eat beans and rice on a regular basis during our debt-slaying journey).

In fact, at the end of our journey, a dinner of rice and beans became a weekly and somewhat spiritual meal. Partaking in such frugal fare allowed us to recall where we had been and look forward to where we were going. Simple meals also gave us a great platform to discuss with our princesses how people eat all over the world. Once again, as we raised our forks, we lifted our praises for being blessed with more than we deserved, even in culinary simplicity.

While paying off debt, you can still enjoy the gift of your favorite meals, even the occasional meal at a restaurant. You just might not be able to enjoy those meals every single day. It's wise to open your hearts and ears to the call of laying down your favorites during the debt-slaying journey. In the final days of our battle, when we felt the call to give up meat for a short period of time, it seemed like a crazy sacrifice.[7] Standing on the other side of the dragon's carcass, it was a temporary (albeit extreme in the eyes of some) calling that I can barely remember. We still had plenty to eat. We still broke and even enjoyed the bread that we were given. But only because God blessed the sacrifice.

When it comes to your royal table, your sturdiest weapon in the battle to slay the debt dragon is intentionality. In every area possible, think through your week before it ever begins. Determine what meals you will have and when you will have them. Strategically base your grocery shopping list on the items you already possess. Place "stops" or commandments in your own way to prevent overspending at the grocery store. Don't waste your money on foods that won't satisfy your body or soul. Don't crack out the "welllllllll" excuses and lies.

Delight in the many good gifts that God has already blessed you with.

 ## Debt-Slaying Strategies

✓ Survey your family's favorites to inform your meal planning process. Using the results, plan at least five meals you could regularly rotate into your weekly meal plan.

✓ Print out the meal planner from QueenofFree.net.

✓ Create your own Grocery Store Top Ten.

✓ Spend thirty minutes on Sunday evening preparing lunch items for the week.

Chapter 6

KEEPING THE CASTLE CLEAN

Cleaning your house while your kids are still growing up
is like shoveling the walk before it stops snowing.
PHYLLIS DILLER

MOST DAYS OF THE WEEK, I'm an absolute mess. I'm not talking about an emotional mess or even a spiritual mess, although there are certainly days when those tags apply too. I am, however, a physical mess. My whole life long, I've struggled to keep my world ordered. I was the kid with the crazy messy desk who never seemed to snag the elusive "Neat as a Pin" award. My locker was actually photographed and documented in my high school yearbook because of its atrociousness. My poor sweet college roommates knew that my closet would regularly throw up my dirty laundry all over the floor.

The King of Free? Let's just say he got swindled when it comes to that whole "for better or for worse" agreement in this area of our marriage. I struggle to keep things straight. I *hate* to clean. I dust twice a year—right before I put out Christmas decor and when I put it away (sometime in late January). If it looks like my house has been cleaned from top to bottom right before you came over, it's because my house was cleaned from top to bottom *right* before you came over. I clean only when we're expecting company or when I'm avoiding some other deadline. Okay, maybe it's not *quite* that bad, but I am no June Cleaver, vacuuming in my heels and pearls. In fact, for a long time, I didn't even have a vacuum that worked, and that was fine with me. (I mean, what's wrong with using a Shop-Vac now and then?)

I'd love to tell you that as we were paying off our debts, I magically began *loving* to do the dishes, clean the toilet, and take out the trash. I would like you to think that I whistle while I work, wearing my cute vintage-styled apron, laboring over each piece of laundry with extra loving care. If I told you that, I'd be a complete and total liar—except for the apron part. I do have two of those. To be honest, the only reasons I clean are so I can wear a cool apron and so my kids won't look like Pigpen from the Peanuts gang when they go to school.

But while our debt-slaying journey didn't spark a sudden passion for cleaning, that experience did teach me how closely paying off debt and keeping a clean castle are linked. I also discovered many ways to save money on everything from laundry to dishes to household appliances. While I am not sure I will actually *ever* enjoy cleaning, I have struck a happy medium in my approach to the systems in our home. Beyond scrubbing toilets and the grout in my 1950s shower—which doesn't ever seem to come clean (suggestions are welcome!)—our family began to focus on reducing the clutter that can and will rule over us all. Stuff breeds stuff. The more we have, the more we want. The systems we have to keep our homes clean and clutter-free say a lot both about who we are and where we are going.

In this chapter I hope to challenge your thinking when it comes to your home. From how much (or how little) you have to the way you pay your bills to maybe even how you wash your clothes, slaying the debt dragon requires a complete paradigm shift. When you begin looking at every aspect of your life as ripe with the potential of eliminating debt, momentum builds. Being willing to make changes in the simplest of ways fuels your journey—and the literal change you save as a result can be used to help you pay off what you owe.

A New World Order

A week before I was due to give birth to our older daughter, Anna, I walked around a full five centimeters dilated. Want to really freak out salesclerks at the mall or grocery store? When they ask how far along you are, answer with that little piece of information. Immediately people will scurry toward the nearest sources of hot water and scissors, thinking they are going to have to deliver your baby. I probably divulged a little too much private information just to see people squirm uncomfortably or at least look at me in utter confusion.

Similarly, if I want to get a rise out of someone who wants to know how we paid off so much debt, I tell them, "I quit my job." While not the full explanation, in many ways this truth was an essential catalyst for our journey. (Wait a minute! Hang up your phone. I did not just instruct you to dial your boss and scream "*I quit!*" into the receiver. What worked for me may not work for you.) In August 2008, about four months into our debt-slaying journey, Brian and I decided it would be best for me to become a stay-at-home mom.

This was incredibly complicated because

1. I *loved* what I was doing and even felt called to my job.
2. I knew I would let down a great number of people outside of my family when I stepped out of my job.
3. Even though the job was part-time in pay, it was helping us whack away at debt.

Despite the apparent drawbacks to quitting my job, my heart, brain, and soul wouldn't let it rest. Not only did I realize that we just might be more effective in paying off debt if I channeled my energies into managing our household well, I also wasn't happy with my response to the question, *If I had hired me to run my home, would I fire myself or give myself a raise?*

The resounding answer was that I would have given myself a big boot and exclaimed, "Don't let the door hit ya on the rear as you exit." I was *not* managing our home well. Though my job was considered part-time, I was working long hours, and I didn't want to cook or plan meals when I got home. We constantly had to wash a small load of laundry just to have something to wear the next morning. I was exceeding the monthly limit on my cell phone plan because of all the work calls I was making. I had to line up child care for our daughters while I attended staff meetings. I had to spend extra money to fill my car with gas and buy work attire. I was purchasing items for my job on our dime, often waiting long periods of time for reimbursements. On top of that, the Princess Youngest was just a few months old and rarely sleeping at night, which was stretching me to my limits mentally, emotionally, physically, and spiritually.

Bedraggled, confused, and overwhelmed, I began to examine our finances and debt-repayment progress. *Could God really be calling me to stay home full-time?* I did the quick-and-dirty math on how much I was bringing home with my part-time job and contrasted it with the "extra" money we were able to pay toward debt because of my part-time income. The totals were nearly identical. That meant if I quit my job, we would still be able to pay the minimums on all of our bills, no problem. We could stay afloat without the aid of credit cards or loans. But we would have no extra funds to devote toward the huge chunk of change that we owed. In other words, after being able to pay off a few small debts in the first four months, we would return to square one.

I began to ask myself several "what if" questions. *What if I ran our home like a business? What if I looked for every possible way to increase our productivity? What if I began streamlining our spending?*

We were already fairly frugal, but what if I investigated ways to reduce spending further? What if I reexamined everything from the utility bills we paid to the toilet paper we were buying and ran every purchase through the filter of the bottom line? If I intentionally managed our home in this way, would I actually make up my part-time income?

Because we had paid off those first small debts in the previous four months, we now had enough cushion in our budget to cover all of our expenses. It gave us the breathing room I needed to take a leap of faith and quit my job. Resigning from something I loved to do was a sacrifice. When I thought about leaving my job, I realized that even though my job was part-time, much of my identity and feelings of worth came

> God can take your passion, no matter how silly it seems, and use it to create a path you never anticipated.

from being successful at it. It was a way for me to express my love for God, and I could see that I was making a difference in people's lives. Walking away meant I would need to lean on God to truly shape who He wanted me to be and to trust that He had a plan for me as I re-imagined how our home would run.

I want to acknowledge again that it's not possible for everyone who is paying off debt to stay at home. Some households are dual income earners by choice; some are by necessity. It was a tough decision, especially given the fact that we had only socked away $1,000 in an emergency fund and paid off three minor debts at that time. But the call on my heart was so strong that I felt I had no choice but to resign.

Oddly enough, that very same month, I had begun the hobby of sharing my love for free stuff on my blog, *Queen of Free*. At the time, I had no idea that this hobby would become a lifeline, a platform, and a unique calling of its own over the next five years. I honestly began simply because I wanted to tell people when to get free sweet tea from Chick-fil-A and free undies from Macy's. It's a prime example of how God can take your passion, no matter how silly it seems, and use it to create a path you never anticipated. And mind you, that path is always marked with much more grace-filled awesomeness than the one you could ever lay out on your own.

Take Charge of Your Utilities

So in September 2008, I laid down my "good" part-time job for what could have seemed like a demotion but ended up being nothing short of a fairy tale. Of course it felt nothing like a fairy tale at the start. It felt hard . . . and lonely . . . and sometimes like complete and total drudgery. But it made a difference.

In those early days, I spent a lot of time focusing on ways we might trim our utility bills. I've found that tidbit seems to surprise many people. After all, when thinking about where to tighten the budget, people often turn first to couponing to trim the grocery budget. If we're incredibly focused, we eliminate the extras of vacations, date nights, and going to the movies. But rarely do we think about what we can do to reduce those monthly expenses that appear to be "set." Certainly we *must* pay utility bills. I like heat. I like light. I like that water comes out of our faucets and that someone comes and takes away our trash every week. Also, I big puffy heart the sewage system because "eww" without it. I fancy using a telephone on occasion, especially for emergencies or to call my mom. It is possible to overpay for these basic, life-giving services, though. In my quest to run our household like a business, I dug through our old bills and read the fine print. We then made some difficult choices about our lifestyle and those monthly bills that some might consider "necessary."

Cable—always first on the chopping block. We had ditched basic cable years prior to beginning our debt-slaying journey. Our choice was based on finances and my complete lack of self-control when it came to watching a marathon of shows on the History Channel. (I know, I know, I am just filled with surprises and thrilling habits, but then again, I did major in history back in college.) To cut back on my intake of documentaries about the six wives of Henry VIII, I called our cable company and requested the "poverty package," which is sometimes referred to as the poor man's package, though anyone can choose this service. While embarrassing, those were probably some of the best words I've ever spoken. For us, this very stripped-down, basic package included local channels and—most importantly for our household of little people—PBS Kids programming. At the time, the price was roughly $12 a month, and the services more than met our needs.

Gradually, the poverty package crept up to a little over $19 a month, and we decided to eliminate it entirely. Luckily, as the years passed, online streaming offerings like Netflix, Hulu, Amazon, and even network websites began offering us many of the options that cable provides. When choosing a streaming service, be sure to take into account both cost and which shows are available. You might also consider any additional benefits. For example, Amazon Prime offers streaming but also two-day shipping as a part of the cost. Netflix and Hulu Plus are billed on a monthly basis, but Amazon requires an annual fee. Netflix best fit our budget and television tastes, but your choice may be different. Don't forget that many networks also offer their shows on the free version of Hulu or the network website. Yes, programs may air a day or even a season late, but the cost savings are worth the wait, I promise. In fact, after breaking the hold that television has on your routine, you might not even miss it.

For a year and a half, we went without local channels. However, after we were debt-free, the King of Free followed a YouTube tutorial and constructed a homemade antenna. We can finally watch NFL games and my weekly news segment without crashing someone else's pad. The antenna cost him a grand total of $3.49 to build (he still has the receipt) and pulls in more channels than we will ever need. It kind of looks like a modern art sculpture of a cat, too. After a wee bit of "debate," *we* decided it would look best sitting on the back deck rather than in the middle of our living room.

As you consider how to scale back or eliminate the television programming in your home, remember that the costs of TV come not only in the form of the monthly bill but also in time wasted and desires created. Instead of watching TV in the evenings, our family often concentrated our time and energy on working from home or building our marriage. We've played more games of Phase 10 than I care to number. Plus, our brains were not constantly bombarded with commercials or movie trailers, letting us know exactly what we were missing out on. Turning off the television just might be your best first step in living a life of contentment and eliminating debt.

I'm certain that switching off the cable might feel like a major sacrifice to members of some families. But while it can stink to have to give up certain things, it's another opportunity to focus on the greater vision of the "why" of your debt-slaying journey. Not only that, but the sacrifice might be only temporary (unless you're like us and decide not to return to it) and is for a greater good. Whether it's the promise of a vacation someday or a college education, help the members of your family dream big dreams in the midst of this change. I promise that after a month or so, the perceived "need" for television will probably slip away. Our older daughter, Anna, became a voracious reader, and our younger daughter, Zoe, discovered she actually preferred the swing set. Our family has read more, played more, and been more active thanks to the flip of a switch.

Leave the lights on for me (and the heat, too). I once heard a fellow debt slayer say that his family had turned off their power to save money. I'll be honest. I'm much more of a pansy than that guy. I like the comforts of the modern world. I live in a climate where heat is required in the winter. My idea of camping is staying in a luxury cabin or a cute B and B before hiking. Pioneers were rock stars, but I'll keep my modern conveniences and cough up the change for the utility bill. However, that doesn't mean I'm not intentional when it comes to energy consumption.

Obviously, you need to monitor your usage of lights and heat. Simply making a daily practice of turning off the lights and, in the winter, adjusting your thermostat to a lower temp at night and when you're not at home will help your bottom line. Also, regularly unplugging small appliances can help you save big bucks. Taken together, space heaters, lamps, toasters, coffee pots, desktop computers, and TVs eat a whole lot more energy than dryers and refrigerators. So take an extra step or two to pull the plug nightly or before you leave home for the day. You can even easily save money by opening your curtains during the day to let in natural light and pulling them shut in the evenings to keep your home well insulated.

I highly recommend seeking out an energy audit, too. An energy professional will walk through your home with you, making suggestions to increase your efficiency (which will decrease your bill). You also often receive a complimentary box filled with lightbulbs, showerheads, sink aerators, and more. Our technician even changed our lightbulbs for us. In most states, it's completely free! Don't forget to seal up cracks and close the vents in your house *before* winter weather arrives too. Setting aside an hour to caulk and apply weather stripping may seem like a hassle, but it will save plenty of money in the long run.

One of the oddest yet simplest energy money-saving tips I've learned is to sweep the dust from the back of your refrigerator. You might as well vacuum the vent at the bottom in the front too. Often these areas clog up with dust and hair. Not only do they look like part of a haunted house, but they also cause problems both for your energy bill and the refrigerator itself. Prolong the life of your appliance while you cut down on kilowatts. I'll wait here for you while you go and do that so we both feel like we accomplished something. (Pause). Oh good, you're back! On to the next utility.

Don't drown in your water bill. Have a leaky faucet or a toilet that runs nonstop? Fix it *now*. Do not waste one second. Your leaks could be doubling your water bill. Even while you are paying off debt, it's worth hiring a professional plumber to fix your water woes. Of course, if you are a DIY whiz, then make the repair yourself. Get on it immediately. If you keep telling yourself that you'll get around to it "one day," your money will literally run down the drain. If your bill suddenly spikes, call the water company straightaway and ask them for an explanation. It's unlikely that your rates will increase astronomically in a month's time, but the company might have some insight into why your bill went up, along with tips to help you make course corrections.

Ring ding, ding dong. Even before we began whacking away at our debt, we had ditched our telephone landline after a family of squirrels chewed through the outside wire. Repeatedly. Even though we're now debt-free, we still use only cell phones. While we were getting out of debt, I chose the plan with the fewest minutes and no texting. Until very recently, I also had an old iPhone that I used while on WiFi. Though we had no data plan, I was able to download a free texting app, and I could connect to WiFi almost everywhere I went. (I admit that I did get strange stares when I attempted to explain that I had one number for calls and another for texts.) After watching prices and finding a sale recently, I received a free smartphone when I signed up for an unlimited talk and text plan that costs less than my previous service. Hooray for finally living in the same decade as everyone else. Hooray, too, for waiting for a very good gift. I appreciate the ability to text and call from the same number, to be able to carry only one phone, and to even be able to use the Internet from time to time much more than I ever would have if I hadn't gone five years without a smartphone. Delayed gratification, bargaining, and intentionality paid off for me.

Shopping around and asking lots of questions about discounts and deals will go far when it comes to managing your phone bill. Repeatedly ask, "Is that *really* the best we can do?" Be kind but firm in your negotiations, and don't be afraid to ask for a manager if you aren't getting anywhere. The worst someone can tell you is no.

Internet. We decided to splurge in this one area. Obviously Internet isn't a necessity to life and can be incredibly expensive. Still, there are ways to control the costs. First, remember that in certain parts of the country, the families of students who receive free or reduced lunch qualify for inexpensive high-speed Internet service. And every one of us can call and ask our cable provider the "Is that *really* the best we can do?" question, which may enable you to save quite a bit on your monthly bill.

When our Internet bill recently crept up another two dollars per month, we considered switching to a fiber optic company. I called our service provider one last time and asked to be transferred to the "retention" or "loyalty" department. These must have been magic words because after another forty minutes on the phone, the company agreed to drop our bill by twenty dollars a month for six months. I know that spending forty minutes of your life on hold may not seem worth it, but if you need an additional $120 to swing at the debt dragon, it turns out to be a pretty good hourly rate.

> Don't fall for the bundling marketing strategy. Convincing yourself that it is *not that much more* per month can doom you.

At a bare minimum, don't fall for the bundling marketing strategy. It might be *only* an additional ten dollars to add cable or even a phone line to your Internet service, but ten dollars a month works out to $120 a year. You *need* that $120 to slay your debt dragon. Small changes can make a big difference. Convincing yourself that it is *not that much more* per month can doom you—especially if you repeat that logic in several areas of your finances. Don't fall for the bundle.

The Laundry List

I like wearing clean clothes. I'm convinced that being handed a towel fresh from the dryer as I step out of the shower is a piece of heaven right here on earth. Combine that towel with a pair of freshly laundered jammies, clean sheets, and my favorite blanket? My world goes into orbit. But as much as I love the luxury that is clean laundry, I despise the actual process of "doing" the laundry.

I know, I know. It's a first-world problem, and people all over the world wash their clothes in a stream, beating them on a rock. I should probably quit my whining and be thankful. The fact remains, however, that I tense up every time I walk past one couch in our home that is almost always piled high with clean laundry. That's right. I will wash the laundry; I will put the laundry in the dryer. I will even take it out of the dryer and neatly fold it. I just have trouble with the "putting it away into drawers" phase.

What's up with that? I might not ever get beyond my laundry quirks, but thankfully, I at least found some ways to save on this "necessary evil" during our debt-slaying journey.

Let everyone own it. You might be a bit like me and make yourself out to be more of a martyr than necessary at home. In my less-than-best moments, I've been known to grumble under my breath that no one else does *anything* to help out. While that might be true, often I haven't asked anyone for help either. Of course, after I let that emotion build up, I eventually blow my top and yell, "*Bring your clothes to the laundry room!*" in a voice unfamiliar to my children (and even a little scary to me). Rather than going to that ugly place, I suggest you begin encouraging your family to pitch in with the laundry on a regular basis.

Eventually I set up four baskets and a hamper in our laundry room for easy sorting—one for brights, one for darks, one for whites, and one for light-colored clothes. The towels and sweaty gym clothes go into the hamper. Even the Princess Youngest (age six) gets in on the "fun" (because it can be fun if you frame it that way). When everyone does their own sorting, life is a wee bit easier for me. Not only is it a time-saving tip; it saves money, too. The less time I spend picking up and sorting laundry, the more time I can spend working on more profitable projects. Bonus: my attitude tends to be better.

One minor piece of advice and a life lesson learned from experience: *Don't try to set a new expectation in the middle of chaos or a problem.* Standing knee deep in towels and underwear in your bathroom isn't the ideal occasion to ~~scream at~~ convince everyone that it's time for a change. Instead, cast the vision during a calm moment outside of the issue at hand.

Don't try to set a new expectation in the middle of chaos or a problem.

Make your own laundry detergent. If I had a nickel for every time someone marveled because we make our own laundry detergent or asked for my recipe, we would have gotten out of debt much more quickly!

I'd like you to think that I'm a frugal superhero and began this process because I knew it would save me lots of money (which it does). However, I was compelled into this practice rather unwillingly. Our family had been loyal to a particular brand of detergent for over a decade, but a change in its formula forced my hand. Everyone was sneezing and sniffling even though I was using the "Original" scent.

I had to find a fragrance-free alternative. I settled on a basic recipe I found on Pinterest that called for one cup of borax, one cup of washing soda,[1] and one cup of grated Ivory soap.[2] After all the ingredients have been mixed together, you just add one to two tablespoons per load. (Typically I go with the higher amount for towels or stinky clothes.)

Here are a few additional tips:

- Yes, you can use your homemade detergent in high-efficiency machines, although it works better if you put it in with the clothes rather than in the dispenser.
- Our washing machine is located in a non-climate-controlled area, so I tend to use the warm or hot setting, especially during the winter months. Otherwise our clothes freeze and the soap doesn't break down as well.
- Although the allergies in our house prevent us from adding much fragrance, you can choose a soap with more scent.
- Most important, our laundered clothes smell clean and appear bright.

Over the years, I've tweaked the recipe a bit. Now I use a half cup of a generic Oxy cleaner in lieu of the grated bar of soap. I typically combine 13 cups of borax, 13 cups of washing soda, and 7½ cups of Oxy cleaner, and mix it in a five-gallon bucket—enough for up to 832 loads! Making such a large batch keeps me out of the store where I would be apt to make other purchases at the same time. Best of all, I save a great deal by making my own detergent, which costs about 1.6 cents per load, compared to 8 cents to 23 cents a load for store-bought detergent.

A few years ago we ran the numbers on how much we save by making our own laundry detergent. We calculated that by the time I'd used up one batch, I had saved between $58 and $166 (depending on the brand) on detergent alone (not counting the impulse buys I might have made when I ran out *just* to get this household essential).

Swap vinegar for fabric softener. Okay, I admit I was skeptical initially. I had latent fears that we would smell like Easter eggs or salad dressing. But I've discovered that white vinegar is a miracle cleaner and a perfect substitute for liquid fabric softeners or dryer sheets. I simply fill a Downy Ball with vinegar rather than softener. Bonus: the vinegar also brightens and whitens clothes. It won't damage your darks, either. We have a set of the spiky dryer balls to help cut down on static and increase the efficiency of the dryer, too.

Hang 'em high. One beautiful summer afternoon, I decided to hang jeans on the curtain rod in our living room and let the lovely breeze blowing through our windows dry them. Since then, we've rarely finished drying a pair of jeans in the dryer. I tend to toss them in the dryer for five to ten minutes to knock the wrinkles out and then hang them upside down on pant hangers in our laundry room (although our "redneck living room clothesline" suits me just fine too). I also dry sweaters or sweatshirts on hangers in the laundry room or lay them flat.

Not only does this cut down on the electric bill, but the fabrics hold up much longer and don't shrink. Because of the aforementioned allergies and Indiana's high pollen count, I doubt we'll ever be poster children for an outdoor clothesline, but the indoor version suits us just fine.

Wash full loads; use cold water. Washing full loads of laundry rather than small loads will dramatically help cut down on your water *and* electric bills. Sometimes, small loads are unavoidable. In particular, the King of Free's dress shirts really need to be laundered in smaller loads or they get mangled and wrinkly. But when you can, fill up the washer—though maybe not too stuffed or you might end up with a repairman at your house. (Oh, that's never happened to you? Um, me neither.)

As I mentioned above, I use warm or hot water during the winter months, but go with cold water whenever I can. It's a tried-and-true money saver.

Don't get taken to the cleaners. Avoid "dry clean only" clothes like the plague. If you have any amount of debt, you don't need someone else doing your laundry for you. Even dry-clean-only items like men's suits don't need to be professionally cleaned more than once per year or the fabric may be damaged.

The King of Free's professional attire looks sharp, and except for that annual trip to the dry cleaner with his suits, he launders it all himself. That's right, ladies, he does his own laundry, and he's all mine. He is also intentional about hanging things up after they've been worn and not letting anything get trampled on the floor.

More Cleaning Solutions

Erma Bombeck once noted, "Housework, if you do it right, will kill you."[3] At this point, you probably realize Erma and I are kindred spirits. I'm not much into any cleaning craze. I do my best, though, to keep things in our home orderly by using some frugal cleaning products. I love that each is not only affordable but also nearly fragrance-free and much more friendly for the environment, too.

White vinegar, the miracle elixir. I'm not sure there's anything white vinegar can't do when it comes to cleaning your home and taking care of your family. It's a disinfectant. It makes awesome window and glass cleaner. It's my go-to fabric softener.

I use it in the rinse dispenser of my dishwasher. I use it to kill weeds. Seriously, Google "white vinegar" and you're sure to find nine million uses.

Baking soda—for more than just chocolate chip cookies. Baking soda, another of the classic cleaners, can be used for nearly everything from homemade toothpaste to carpet deodorizer. If one of your kiddos is prone to car sickness, it can work miracles at removing those odors too. (Experience, yo.)

Scrub your toilets and sinks with baking soda, or in the weirdest of twists, make a paste by combining it with water to relieve itching or bee stings. Find it in the well-known small box in the baking aisle or in bulk in the cleaning aisle. We keep a box on the stove top for my cooking "mishaps" too. Probably one of the oddest cleaners I've concocted with baking soda is a homemade jewelry cleaner that left my wedding ring gleaming.[4]

Rubbing alcohol. Removing ink stains, cleaning hairspray off mirrors, keeping your windows frost-free during the winter, and even dispelling fruit flies are in rubbing alcohol's bag of tricks. It's incredibly inexpensive and typically located in the pharmacy. A simple Google search reveals there are many more uses that I've never tried before too.

Borax. There is nothing new under the sun. Borax has been used to clean homes since the late 1800s. This naturally occurring mineral can be used to fight odors and stains, scour and shine pots and pans, wash dishes, and cut grease. You will find borax in the laundry detergent aisle of your grocery store or big box retailer. Look for it near the powdered detergent.

Many of its uses and recipes for cleaning are right on the box. It's a key ingredient in both my laundry detergent and dishwashing detergent recipes.[5]

Washing soda. It's easy to confuse washing soda with baking soda; after all, Arm & Hammer makes both. Washing soda has a bit more oomph, and it sudses up too. Again, it's found in the laundry detergent aisle, is all natural, and makes a great detergent booster to give any laundry soap extra cleaning power. It can also be combined to make your own home cleaners. It plays a featured role in our dishwashing detergent recipe.

Reusable towels, bottles, and scrubbers. Rather than purchasing products that will be pitched in the trash after one use, try using reusable towels, squirt bottles, and sponges or scrubbers with multiple-use potential. While we were paying off debt, I rarely purchased paper towels or other consumable goods. Instead I tried to use towels that could be washed and reused. Sheets of newspaper make a great alternative to paper towels for cleaning windows and mirrors, too.

Boiling water. Have a slow drain? Soap scum built up on your shower walls or sink? Your first line of defense should always be a teakettle filled with boiling water. That's right—for a penny or less you might be able to take care of your problem without even purchasing a cleaning product. Look at you go!

The cleaning product aisle is filled with items you simply don't need. Coupons for new cleaning products clog your Sunday paper, but more than likely, the same basic, earth-friendly products that your great-grandmother used will work for you, too. If possible, avoid going down the cleaning product aisle altogether so you don't know exactly what you're "missing out on."

New Eyes for a New You

Frugality has long been considered a spiritual discipline. It is profitable, too. Frugality will help you

> rid yourself and your home of excess
> manage your home more effectively
> reduce the amount of cleaning you need to do
> bless someone else

Thriftiness means looking at every item in your house with new eyes. How could you use it again? Could it be a blessing to someone else? Could you sell it to pay off debt? Do you really need it? These are vital questions in maintaining your home.

> **Thriftiness means looking at every item in your house with new eyes.**

Say one has a particular passion for books. (I'm not talking about anyone in particular. Or someone who may have typed these words. Just a hypothetical situation, you know.) Anyway, such a person could look at the many books lining her shelves and begin to ask a couple of key questions about each volume: (1) Will I read it again? (2) Would I want to keep it to loan it to someone else? If the answer to both of these questions is no, that "hypothetical person" would probably either want to donate or sell that book.[6]

Maybe you're not a bibliophile but have amassed way more of something else than you need. Reducing the number of toys, bowls, blankets, dishes, books, clothes, shoes, or [fill in the blank] in your house is sure to lighten your load. You will have less to manage and less to keep clean. Fewer dishes in your cabinet will equal fewer dishes to wash. Fewer toys in the closet will equal fewer painful moments after stepping on them in the middle of the night. Fewer clothes in your drawers will mean less laundry. Seriously, how could anyone advocate against less laundry?

Clearing the clutter may give you the opportunity to be a huge blessing to someone else. After all, slaying the debt dragon doesn't mean you can't be generous. *As you pay off debt, you must realize that you—like almost everyone else in our nation—have an abundance of blessings.* Practicing frugality means that sometimes you will be blessed with the opportunity to get creative with how you give. Honestly, in some ways giving money can be easy. It requires little forethought or personal effort. Sure, there is always pain in parting with cash. However, giving away your "things" can be much more difficult and require more of you. I'm not talking about the shirt with a stain on it or the shoes that no one would want to wear. Sometimes we are called to lighten our load both to bless others and to give ourselves breathing room. You may have to change your lens on what you believe generosity to be, though. Maybe you'll be called to give up your stuff. Maybe you'll feel led to give up your time. Whatever the call, looking beyond what you don't have helps you focus on your goal of kicking debt in the teeth.

Two Christmases ago, a friend of mine sent out a plea on behalf of a refugee community living in our midst. Recently relocated, many of these families lacked the most basic household items. Immediately I sprang into action. Digging through the back corners of my cabinets, I cleared out an entire eighteen-gallon plastic tote of kitchenware in less than thirty minutes. The number of dishes, bowls, measuring cups, baking pans, and kitchen gadgets that we either had duplicates of or had never used was embarrassing. You know what? Since giving

DEBT-SLAYING DUO

PETER AND JEN, 32 AND 36 | **PAID OFF $107,100;**
debt-free, including their mortgage

Peter and Jen are our debt-free heroes. Brian and I long for the day when we can include the mortgage in our debt-free total. I hope their story inspires you as much as it does us.

Why slay the debt dragon?

When Peter and Jen got married in 2006, they started off their lives together without any debt except a mortgage. Jen had purchased a home in 2005 and rounded up her mortgage payment an even hundred dollars from the get-go. In 2008, this dynamic duo decided to try living on one income for their regular expenses, allocating extra dollars to the mortgage. They then calculated what their house would cost over the duration of a thirty-year loan. Even with a low-interest mortgage, they realized their home would end up costing more than double the original loan amount if taken to term. They said this discovery was "simultaneously ridiculous and truly motivating!" They knew they wanted to put the money they were earning outside of monthly living expenses toward paying off their mortgage. In 2013, they reached their goal of paying off their home, owning it free and clear in eight years and one month. What a relief to slice off the thousands of dollars' worth of interest they would have paid had they taken it to term.

What surprised them most about paying off debt?

A huge loan shrinks quicker than you think it can when you focus on paying it down. You need to know where your money goes, which definitely requires budgeting. Peter and Jen were also shocked at the contentment eliminating their mortgage brought. "When we paid off our house, the desire to move into a bigger house and take on another mortgage faded. This is ours now! It may not be big. It may not be fancy. But even if we both lost our jobs, we would still have a place to live. That feeling is very comforting."

What kept them going?

Peter and Jen carefully tracked where extra money went while committing to work long hours. Anytime their balance decreased, they felt an emotional high. Together they created a chart and a graph, showing how long it would take to pay off their loan. Every time an extra payment was made, the line got steeper, which indicated a closer pay-off date. Making that line steeper and steeper became a game for this pair. Combating debt together further encouraged teamwork in their marriage.

How did they celebrate?

After slaying their debt dragon, Peter and Jen hosted a mortgage-burning party. Once popular, such celebrations are nearly unheard of in the United States now. During the 1970s and 1980s, mortgage-burning parties even made their way into television episodes. Characters on *Eight Is Enough*, *All in the Family*, and *M*A*S*H* all celebrated paying off their homes. Peter and Jen happily brought this tradition back in style. Gathering together friends, they served a delicious meal and then brought everyone outside to literally burn the mortgage documents. They had their friends write the names of their favorite charities on slips of paper, which were then placed in a jar. The name of one charity was drawn at random, and Peter and Jen donated the amount that would have been their next mortgage payment to that charity. In addition to the party with friends, the pair celebrated with a nice dinner out on their own.

Their encouragement and advice for you

"Society might say a mortgage is normal and paying off your house is *impossible*," says this dynamic duo. "Make slaying that mortgage your goal, then focus on it and budget to see what *impossible* feats you accomplish!"

Peter and Jen suggest following some of the same concrete steps they took to fuel your own debt-slaying journey:

- Cut out cable TV.

- Drive old cars.

- Pay with cash.

- Visit the ATM only once a month.

- Live in a small house, so you are less tempted to buy stuff because you have no place to put it.

The catalyst that launched Peter and Jen's journey was the bottom line. They encourage you to use a mortgage calculator to estimate exactly how much you will end up paying if you take your mortgage to term. That number might surprise and motivate you at the same time.

Peter and Jen attest to the fact that even the smallest "extra" payment can make a big difference. Paying an extra $100 early in your mortgage is like doubling your money—the $100 goes toward your principal, saving you around $100 in interest. Rather than focusing on what you can't do, channel your energies toward making a small difference over time.

How has paying off debt changed their marriage?

Peter says, "Paying off debt gave us a joint project to work on, something we could battle against shoulder to shoulder. It gave us a common purpose and goal. Every financial discussion became easier and easier. After paying off $100K, it is pretty much impossible to have 'money fights' anymore. What is there to argue about?" Jen adds, "Once you take on a financial goal together, talking about money and budgeting becomes second nature. The *budget* word loses all its scariness and negative connotations."

them away, I haven't missed or felt the need to replace any of those items. I've had fewer dishes to wash and fewer "things" to manage. Plus, I prayed over those items before I handed them off to my sweet friend. I prayed that the items would be put to good use by people who really *needed* them, knowing whoever received them would find them to be more useful than just back-of-the-cabinet "stuff."

Lest you think me some sort of saint, I must confess that I still pray to be delivered from debt every single day.

> Every time a thought of wanting something we can't afford
> sneaks into my soul.
> Every time a desire to spend recklessly assaults my heart.
> Every time I want to blame my spouse for my own errors.
> Every time I want the world to throw me a pity party because
> we choose to make a difficult financial decision.
> Every time I make a mistake with money.
> Every time I choose my own wants and needs over those I know
> God has called me to seek out.

It's in those times that I often remember a favorite Scripture of mine: "A person without self-control is like a house with its doors and windows knocked out" (Proverbs 25:28). Once you've pared your belongings or blessed someone else with your abundance, you *must not* purchase more items to replace what you've sold or given away. This requires extreme self-control. *Self-control is a hedge around your soul.*

Proverbs 25:28 points out that when we lack self-control, we leave ourselves incredibly vulnerable. Anything or anyone can sweep into our "windows and doors," robbing us blind. The winds blow easily through our home, completely destroying what is inside. Our families are left without protection from the physical elements of life. And we're left wide open to the schemes of the thief who comes to "steal and kill and destroy" us all (John 10:10, NLT).

Plain and simple, while none of it was grand or expensive, Brian and I came to realize that we had too much stuff. The more we continue to give away, the more we refine and value what we have. Yes, even though we're debt-free, we still fight the battle against accumulation every single day. We strive to purchase only items we truly love and need. As a result, our household runs much more efficiently. Plus we have more actual money left in our pockets to give away, save, or invest because we're not swept up in the culture of needing that new and improved, next best thing.

Delayed gratification is a virtue that may leave you with less stuff but certainly more self-control. Scrubbing your home clean, in fact, might be more of a spiritual practice than you realized when you began your debt-slaying journey.

Debt-Slaying Strategies

✓ Evaluate your utility bills. Choose one to renegotiate or eliminate this week.

✓ Endeavor to make your own laundry detergent. Either use my recipe or search for one online.

✓ Employ one of the frugal cleaning methods listed this week.

✓ Find five items you can give away to bless others today.

Chapter 7

FORMIDABLE FOES AND FELLOW DEBT SLAYERS

Be completely humble and gentle; be patient, bearing with one another in love.
Make every effort to keep the unity of the Spirit through the bond of peace.

EPHESIANS 4:2-3, NIV

I ENVY THE Princess Youngest's imagination. It is filled with the most delightful places and people. From a wily imaginary friend named Pistachio to adventures in song and dance, she needs very little entertainment outside of her own fancy. If she has an idea or a theory of life rooted deep in her whimsical world, it's very difficult for her to (ahem) adjust to any other ideas.

For example, I had a bear of a time trying to explain that the song "The Bare Necessities" was not actually called "The Bare Miss Stephanie." Her preschool Sunday school teacher's name was set to this unfortunate and slightly embarrassing lyric over and over again. Poor Miss Stephanie.

Misunderstandings and confusion among preschoolers are cute, filled with charm and giggles. Misunderstandings and confusion among adults are much less adorable. Time and time again during our journey of paying off debt, Brian and I were met with bewildered and perplexed expressions and questions.

Why would you want to do that?
Does it really make a difference?
I don't understand.

Those questions were typically followed with disbelief or counterstrategies.

Do you really think you'll be able to do that?
What you really should do is invest all of that money instead of
*   using it to pay off debt.*
Why don't you just use a zero-percent finance plan to buy it now?

As you begin budgeting and implementing some of the cost-cutting strategies we've discussed in the previous chapters, you'll likely be mocked and ridiculed too, perhaps even by members of your own family and by people whom you think of as your friends. The loudest advice, in fact, will most likely come from people who know the least about finance and who manage their own resources poorly.

Some of your critics may be jealous as they see you making progress. Others may be uneasy about their own current financial position but unwilling to sacrifice or to even consider that they could find a way out of their situation. It's not too surprising, given what passes as financial "common wisdom" in our culture:

You don't want your kids to feel deprived and different from
    their classmates.
You should always follow your dreams, no matter the cost.
Everyone has a car payment.

New is always better than used; name brands are always of
    better quality than generics.

College is impossible without student loans.

There's no need to pay anything off before term.

Before you go all nasty on the haters, realize that the majority of your detractors actually come from a good place. They are simply befuddled by your goal to pay off and then stay out of debt. After

Keep Your Eyes on Your Own Paper
January 2011 blog post

It is absolutely essential that you keep a laser-sharp focus on your own personal debt-slaying journey. I say this because when I hear of others paying off debt, I can be encouraged.

Sometimes.

But other times, the green-eyed monster in me begins to make comparisons.

Did they really pay that off?
Did they inherit some cash?
Worse yet, did they take out another loan to pay off that loan/
    credit card/debt?
I bet they make a lot more money than we do.

Or on the opposite end of the spectrum:

How in the world can they afford that?!
We're barely making it, and we could never go there!
Why do people who live irresponsibly seem blessed in spite
    of it?

I can't answer any of these questions. I can't know anyone else's debt load (unless they tell me). I can't know what their payments are like. And bottom line, I don't really need to know any of the above. *It's none of my business.*

Their story is not my story. And neither is my story your story.

And so if someone pays off close to $25,000 in one year and you only make $30,000, there is *absolutely* no reason for you to be discouraged, quit, give up, or think that you can't make it out of debt.

Or if someone goes on a fantastic vacation to Disney°World and the envy monster sets in for you, let it go. You never know if they saved, paid cash, or someone gifted the trip to them.

Again, it's not your road to travel. It's not your battle to fight. It's not the path you have embarked upon.

It's not your story.

Your story is uniquely yours. It is beautifully yours. Your debt-slaying victory won't hinge on anyone else either. That story belongs to you too.

Eyes on your own paper or straight ahead, debt slayers. And chin up. You really don't want anyone else's story or life.

....

all, our culture teaches us not only that debt is okay but also that it's a necessary part of life. Some so-called financial experts even claim you need some "good debt" to be successful in personal finance. The "good debt" concept springs from the notion of financing "anything you need but can't afford to pay for up front without wiping out cash reserves or liquidating all your investments."[1] In other words, as long as you can afford the monthly payments, it's fine to borrow.

There are two traps in this thinking. The first is assuming that you'll always be able to afford the monthly payments. Life is uncertain. I've seen too many people borrow beyond their means and then suffer a job loss or a tragedy, only to discover that their "affordable" monthly payments are suddenly anything but affordable. The second trap is failing to consider the amount of interest that must be paid on purchases that we cannot currently afford. It's possible to end up paying for an item two to three times over once interest is factored in. Make a late payment and you can be socked with penalties and sometimes years' worth of interest on "zero percent" financing plans. One of the most sobering points of our journey was when I discovered that even with an extremely low interest rate, if we took our biggest student loans to term, we would end up paying nearly double the amount. Double a couple of bucks and the impact seems minimal. Double eighty grand and you're staring at an amount commensurate to a nice home you will never live in.

Of course, plenty of people have successfully navigated "good debt" and "payment plans" without scars or tragedy. They might admit that they paid more in interest than they would have liked, but they were still able to afford the payments. With such easy access to payment plans, financing, loans, and credit cards, it's easy to understand why so many people are confused or even critical of those who commit to paying off debt. Yet those same "convenient" payment options carry more risk than Brian and I would ever want to take on again.

But let's be honest. You and I have probably been someone else's detractor at one point in time. Prior to our debt-slaying journey, a friend from high school told me that her husband had her pay off her credit cards before they married. He also insisted that they purchase cars only with cash. I remember thinking, *What a jerk! What ever happened to true love?* My next thought was, *Who pays cash for a car? Is it even possible to save up that much money?* Today I realize that her husband loved her so much that he made financial unity in their marriage a priority, even before they walked down the aisle. That really is "true love." Now that my family has bought a car paying only cash, I realize that *we* are that family that saves up money before buying a vehicle.

Relationships and money are knit so tightly together that it is impossible to separate the two without creating a ridiculous mess. The ways we spend money can be deeply emotional. The practices and philosophies of personal finances are deeply rooted in our past and upbringing. Sometimes friendships are based on how and where and how much we spend. It's no wonder, then, that in-laws, outlaws, and everyone in between will have opinions about your quest to slay the debt dragon. Thinking through how you will address others' reactions *before* they happen will redouble your passion for paying off debt and prevent detractors from sending you spiraling off course—particularly when they imply that you've adopted a bizarre lifestyle.

You Have to Be a Little Crazy

I like to think that my lens on the world is a little unique. I'm suspicious of fads and anyone who tells me I simply *must* read or watch or eat anything. And of course, as the Queen of Free, I'm not afraid to wear a plastic crown out in public or on TV. Want to stand out in a crowd or have people ask you what your story is? Wear a tiara. I promise it's an instant conversation starter. Plus, each time I wear that plastic crown, I am reminded of the importance of our journey— where we have been and where we are going. Sure I looked a little ridiculous, but in the eyes of many, our goals *were* ridiculous. Maybe crazy comes easily for me? Perhaps the craziest thing our family has ever done was endeavor to pay off so much debt. The second craziest was telling the world that we were doing it.

Realize that just by beginning a debt-slaying journey, you, too, will make some people question your sanity. In fact, when you begin fighting to take back financial control, you will need to assume a whole new mind-set. You may have to begin thinking differently in two key ways.

1. **You must be willing to let go of wanting to be like everyone else.** Except in extraordinary circumstances (e.g., that rich great-uncle you never even knew you had leaves you his million-dollar estate), you will need to make sacrifices as you take on your debt. That is likely to lead to some skewed assumptions, such as:

Everyone else vacations.

Everyone else sees movies when they premiere, not a year later when you can rent them for a dollar (or not see them at all).

Everyone else sets their thermostat at a comfortable temperature.

Everyone else throws extravagant birthday parties for their kids.

Everyone else goes to the theme park during the summer.

Everyone else plays travel sports.

Everyone else decorates their home for every season.

Everyone else goes out to fancy restaurants on date nights.

Everyone else buys from every fund-raiser.

Everyone else . . . (you get the point).

It helps to remember that we see only the parts we want for ourselves. From the outside looking in, we typically see only the shiny, happy parts of other people's lives. It's a very one-dimensional view where the sun is always shining and no one has an off day. There's a darker side to "everyone else," too.

Don't forget that "everyone else" may feel absolutely stretched to their financial limits. Everyone else may be using plastic to pay for what they cannot truly afford. Everyone else may not be able to help their children pay for college either. Everyone else may be one paycheck away from not being able to afford the mortgage. Everyone else may need to depend on their children to take care of them during retirement because they have not planned wisely. Everyone else may be contemplating bankruptcy because it feels like their only hope. Being like everyone else isn't all it's cracked up to be. *Paying off debt means you have to let go of wanting to be like everyone else.*

2. **You must be willing to question** *everything.* Every bill, every possession, every tradition, every notion about what is necessary in your life—each must now be scrutinized. Is this a want rather than a true need? Can we sell it? Can we go without? Can we reduce the plan? Can we scale back? Your answer won't always be yes; however, merely changing your mind-set about what you truly *need* brings great freedom.

> Merely changing your mind-set about what you truly *need* brings great freedom.

Thinking through difficult questions will help you see areas where you may have been deceived into doing what everyone else does, resulting in the same financial trials that everyone else now faces too (even if they don't talk about it).

If someone calls you crazy during your pursuit of paying off debt, be encouraged. My guess is you are doing something right.

A True Friend Will Love You Regardless

I love my friends. I have friends with whom I have ridden over 150 miles on bikes in one day. I have friends who have bungee jumped with me. I have friends who visited me in the hospital right after I'd given birth. We have taken classes together. We have studied God's Word together. We have played Just Dance together. We have read books together. We have laughed until we cried together. We have cried until we laughed together. I love my friends.

But no friendship is worth torching your financial future for. If your debt-slaying journey is to be successful, you may need to have a difficult conversation or two . . . or four . . . or sixteen with your friends. Especially if your favorite activities with those friends have included dining out, shopping excursions, and giving each other elaborate gifts. If that's the case, you'll need to redefine your relationship, knowing that redefinition might lead to a schism. It might cause hurt feelings. It might cause tears. In the end, you may have to decide which is worth more to you: a friendship or financial freedom.

Don't misunderstand me. I know that people are worth much more than paying off debt. I also realize that this point is much simpler to make in print than it is to work out in everyday life. Yet relationships that revolve around consumerism merely scratch the surface of what true friendship can be. Your friends are a reflection of what you truly value.

Step back and take a long, hard look at the people you hang around with. Studies show that everything from your body size to the way you approach money can be determined by the people with whom you keep

No friendship is worth torching your financial future for.

company.[2] I love how Craig Groeschel puts it: "Show me your friends and I will show you your future."[3]

Basically, you need a bit of fearlessness to pay off debt. It's not a devil-may-care sort of attitude because you still want to take into account others' feelings. However, you will need to grow some thick skin if someone's ridiculing you. You may even need to be willing to cut ties with those who will either lead you astray or bring you down.

Expecting all your friends to wholeheartedly cheer you on as you begin your debt-slaying journey is one mistake you might make. Another is to simply write them all off. Before finding yourself in a reactive situation, ask your friends for their support. Heartfelt, honest words and the simple request "Can you help me?" will take you far in your friendships.

This might be an incredibly difficult and uncomfortable conversation to initiate. So many of us have grown up in a culture where money—especially a mismanagement or lack thereof—simply isn't discussed outside the walls of our homes. It's embarrassing to admit we have made mistakes, even if we are currently on a path to correct them. Can I embolden you to be brave enough to share with your closest friends that you're endeavoring to pay off debt? Be prepared to explain why you're choosing to do so. Be prepared to explain the how, too. Be prepared to receive advice and nod and smile if it's wacky, without changing your course. Also be prepared for a potential break in your relationship. Some friends may quit calling. If you want to maintain that relationship, then you will need to be more intentional about planning time together that doesn't require spending scads of cash.

Finally, you just might make new friends as you seek to defeat debt, your common foe. The more momentum Brian and I gained in paying off debt, the more we "seemed" to run into people who were on the same path. What a blessing that was, since we all need a community of like-minded travelers to encourage us in our journey, to celebrate our accomplishments, and to motivate us when we feel we're going off track.

Whether with new friends or friends of many years, creating community is an overwhelmingly important part of your debt-slaying journey. We found it in the community group we belong to at our church. Nearly every Thursday night for the past seven years, we've gathered together to study, pray, and encourage one another. We go Christmas caroling every year in the same nursing home. We attend the ball games of one anothers' kids and have the most amazing pitch-in dinners on the planet. We have listened to fantastic speakers together. We have read powerful books together. We have made it our driving purpose to help one another be better parents, better spouses, and better followers of Jesus. Plus, we laugh a lot.

For years, the members of that group were our biggest cheerleaders as we struggled to dig ourselves out of debt. The day after we made our final payment to Sallie Mae, we attended our weekly community group meeting. When we arrived, we were greeted with a cake that had the word *Freedom* piped across the top. The cake was a simple one from the grocery store, but it was the best cake I've ever tasted. Together we toasted God's goodness over glasses of sparkling cider.

That group knows us so well. They've been cheering for us for many years. They have walked with us consistently. Even when they thought we were crazy (surely at some point, they must have), they never voiced those thoughts. They didn't ask us to do things that were outside of our budget. I'm sure they must have wanted to from time to time. They never asked, "Why would you want to do that?" Instead, they encouraged us, prayed for us, asked how things were going, and even gave us hand-me-downs on a regular basis.

Bottom line, you need a supportive group of people (whether or not they're slaying debt themselves) who believe in you as you pay off your debt. You need cheerleaders who are invested in your story and who want to see you win. You need those who will celebrate the small and huge victories of your journey. Just as important, you need to find someone else to root for. Rather than begging for someone else to cheer for you or whining because no one else understands how hard it is, find someone else fighting the same battle.

When we were facing off against the debt dragon, Brian and I gained focus and energy by encouraging others who were in a similar battle. It makes sense, I guess. In a former life, I was a cheerleader— you know, the kind who wears a short, pleated skirt, shakes pom-poms, and kicks her legs up ridiculously high. Nothing energizes me more than applauding someone else's drive and efforts.

Yet you and I don't need pom-poms or a megaphone to be cheer-leaders for other people. We just need to offer simple, straight-up encouragement—via phone, text, social media, written word, or face-to-face communication. It's amazing how sharing stories about victories and battle wounds can lift us up. Laughing over our newest penny-pinching ploy and dreaming about the day we'll be free helps us persevere.

Become someone's superfan. Remind them that *they can do this!* Emphasize the importance of working together with their spouse to overcome financial burdens. Share a time when you were discouraged and what turned it around for you. Follow the apostle Paul's admonition: "Speak encouraging words to one another. Build up hope so you'll all be together in this, no one left out, no one left behind. I know you're already doing this; just keep on doing it" (1 Thessalonians 5:11).

Finding a group of like-minded debt slayers will make all the difference in your journey. At a bare minimum, join the "court" of the Queen of Free on Facebook and Twitter. There, thousands of people daily encourage each other to push through the challenges of paying off debt and share ways to save money. Courses like Dave Ramsey's Financial Peace University and Crown Financial Ministries' Journey to Financial Freedom, which are often hosted by churches, will likely be filled with people just like you, too.[4] Be bold and sign up to learn something while building relationships with other travelers on a similar debt-slaying journey.

Blood Is Thicker than Water

If your friends bring you down as you endeavor to slay your debt dragon, my advice—while not emotionally easy—is not complex: get new friends. Replacing unsupportive family members is, how shall I say, a wee bit trickier. How do you navigate the territory of paying off debt with an extended family that opposes your journey?

For starters, remember that your family's detraction may come from a place of goodwill or even complete confusion. If you have pursued a lifestyle of accumulation until recently, your course correction may befuddle those who are closest to you. Consider how crazy your family would think you were if, after thirty years of never taking a puff, you suddenly started smoking four packs of cigarettes a day. A paradigm shift like that would make any of us seem absolutely insane.

Your family members might also be struggling with their current financial situations. *Shining a light on your own darkness may make others uncomfortable about their lives.* Pursuing excellence in any area of your life will make others either apologize for or rationalize their own behavior. Train to run a marathon and people will automatically share their latest injuries or reasons why they could *never* run. Commit yourself to raising money for a nonprofit and you'll hear why your friends or family are just so busy they would *never* have time to do something like that. Make a nutritional shift and you'll learn why someone else couldn't possibly give up that food or beverage. Even those who say nothing may hope that you'll give up your quest and join them in their never-never land.

> Shining a light on your own darkness may make others uncomfortable about their lives.

Let's be honest, Money-Saving Lords and Ladies, we have *all* done this. We have all been detractors when loved ones do something we just don't understand.

When our own extended families don't seem to get what we're doing and why, our love needs to be more than a surface emotion. We may need to have some difficult conversations about where we are financially and why we're taking what may seem to be drastic steps. Words of encouragement and honesty lead to reconciliation; accusatory tones and threats lead only to broken relationships. That doesn't mean we back down from making the tough financial choices. Sometimes the best way to love someone is to distance ourselves from the person who cannot or will not support us.

You might even be surprised by what you thought was going to be a difficult discussion. I can remember having conversations with both of our brothers' families early on during our debt-slaying journey, explaining that we would need to scale back on our Christmas giving. We'd been worried that our meager twenty-five-dollar budget for their entire family would offend them, but they responded not with hostility but with relief. They were glad to reduce how much they were spending at Christmas too. A simple situation that I expected to cause strife and grief actually brought unity. Sometimes the conversations we create in our heads are worse than reality. Sometimes they aren't.

If you and extended family members can't come together on this issue, perhaps the best thing you can do is say thank you for any areas where they do support you. Expressing gratitude always strengthens relationships, particularly when things have been torn asunder.

Never sacrifice your pursuit of financial freedom in an effort to keep the peace in your extended family. Instead, frame your words around the perspective that seeing the world differently is not incompatible with family unity. Stand firm in your convictions while you love your family well.

I'm Talkin' about Yo' Mama & Yo' Daddy

I've never really liked "yo' mama" or "your mom" jokes. I like them even less now that I am someone's mom. No matter how scarred the relationship, we all struggle with jabs made at our parents. Mind you, we can dole out the jabs ourselves, but when someone else begins to talk smack about our mama or our daddy, the ugly comes out.

Perhaps it's the fact that deep down, we all long to receive affection from our parents. We long to love them and to know they love us, unconditionally. It's no wonder that we may struggle most when our parents don't understand our resolve to get out of debt. It also explains why it can be so hard to break free from the spending, saving, and borrowing patterns they passed down to us.

We inherit so much from our parents. From the color of our eyes to our lens on the world, both the genetics and environment our parents provided filter down into everything we do—including how we view or handle money. Certainly, we need to own our mistakes. If we spent our entire lives blaming someone else for our woes, we'd never move beyond our current circumstances. I'll be the first to admit that our mistakes with money had little to do with either set of our parents. Brian and I created our own drama. However, I'd be remiss if I didn't realize that so much of the way I approach spending and giving comes from my upbringing.

In my case, this was a huge gift. My parents have always been incredibly generous givers, often blessing others in secret. (Oops, I let their secret out.) I inherited this financial "gene" and derive great joy from replicating their behavior. I also always love purchasing a new outfit for my girls when they have an upcoming field trip or other special occasion because I remember my mom frequently doing the same for me. Spending money in this way is certainly meant to be a blessing, but if we don't have the budget to support this generosity, it becomes a curse. It wasn't my best plan when we were $127K in debt, that's for sure. Still, if your parents were wise stewards of their finances, you might turn to them for advice and insights on how to navigate tough financial issues.

My parents fueled our debt-slaying journey in a number of ways. Two in particular stand out in my memory. They sent Brian and me to a leadership conference in 2009. The encouragement and inspiration we received there kept us moving forward. When one of our vehicles died a couple of years into paying off debt, they gave us a truck. Now, it was a well-loved, "charming" sort of vehicle with plenty of miles and character-building features like no air conditioning, a door that would open only if you rolled down the window and used the outside handle, and windshield wipers that operated selectively. Even with its quirks and 210,000 miles, we still affectionately refer to it as our $127K truck. The momentum we gained by not having to purchase another vehicle was just the support we needed.

Maybe your parents haven't been able to offer you such practical support. Maybe they influenced you to manage money in a way that wasn't as positive as the example my parents left me. Maybe your dad hoarded every penny earned, not spending even when it was necessary. Maybe your mom was constantly adding to her collection of credit cards. Maybe they told you all the wrong things about money. Maybe they told you nothing at all. I have no idea what influence your upbringing wields over your current financial situation. But it's a good idea to begin thinking about what you may have intentionally or unintentionally inherited from your parents when it comes to finances. If you are married, then you have at least two sets of parents to consider when it comes to these money genes.

The good news is that even if your parents struggled to practice financial wisdom, you are not doomed to repeat their mistakes. It might also mean that you won't want to consult them for advice on how to handle your household budget. However, when you realize that everyone—including your mom and dad—was influenced in their approach to handling money by their own parents, it may be easier for you to extend grace to them, even when they respond to your efforts with confusing or unkind words.

> **Be firm in your convictions while gentle in your approach.**

This is good to keep in mind when discussing finances with anyone: When you question their practices with money, you might just be questioning their parents' methods. When you discuss your strategies for money management, you might be rattling their foundational understanding of the world, instilled by their parents. This is a very delicate and tender area of intimacy, so I'd admonish you to be firm in your convictions while gentle in your approach.

Not so long ago, I was chatting with a young woman I'll call Jenny who is in the process of merging her finances with her husband's. For many years, they've had separate checking accounts. She feels called to combine their money, and her husband does too. It's been an endeavor of love but not one without struggle. You see, Jenny's stepfather kept a tight fist on the money in her home growing up. She witnessed her mother painstakingly attempt to secure basic household items for their family without much say in how money was spent. Jenny told me, with tear-stained eyes, "I don't know why it's so hard for me to combine our accounts." You can't ignore that how your parents handled money affects the way you handle money, for better or worse. But we all *have* to move beyond those influences at some point (unless every instance was stellar, which is doubtful since our parents are indeed human). My words of encouragement to Jenny, a sweet, vulnerable, truth-seeking, money-saving lady, were rather simple: "He's not your dad."

You see, Jenny's husband is wonderful and trustworthy. He's proven that. She knows that and is in the process of letting go of her past. She has something to teach all parents too. If you have children, realize that their eyes are on you at all times (more on that in the next chapter). They're not just learning from what you say. *As parents, your lives speak more than your words ever will.* So your spending habits, your saving habits, and your attitudes toward money will be passed along just as surely as your dimples and bright blue eyes.

Final Words of Warning

Money-Saving Lords and Ladies, with everything I have in me, I beg you, don't be an obnoxious debt slayer. It is very easy to be so caught up in the passion and success of paying off debt that you begin to tell everyone you know how to handle their finances. Your mom, your best friend, your coworker, your entire social media following are all at risk. When you see yourself as the source of all truth, you are in danger of burning bridges and losing valuable relationships. On top of that, if you start spouting off, "The Queen of Free paid off $127K in debt, and she says . . . ," people will *hate* me. My delicate ego simply cannot handle that. So let's keep your exchanges positive and focus on your own changed behavior rather than what everyone else should do.

Perhaps Jesus put it best:

> Don't pick on people, jump on their failures, criticize their faults—unless, of course, you want the same treatment. That critical spirit has a way of boomeranging. It's easy to see a smudge on your neighbor's face and be oblivious to the ugly sneer on your own. Do you have the nerve to say, "Let me wash your face for you," when your own face is distorted by contempt? It's this whole traveling road-show mentality all over again, playing a holier-than-thou part instead of just living your part. Wipe that ugly sneer off your own face, and you might be fit to offer a washcloth to your neighbor.
>
> MATTHEW 7:1-5

Ouch, right? I know I have sneered way too many times in my life. Most times, it has come back around to bite me in the rear, too, just like that boomerang of criticism. While the words you speak might be true, they are not always helpful. They are not always kind. They are not even always noble. Question your motives before speaking. Then question them again. The people who began to follow our example of paying off debt did so because we encouraged them, not because we used shame and guilt to convince them of their evil ways.

Even so, I suspect plenty more people were turned off by my puppylike excitement in those early days. Instead of measuring my words, I bulldozed over others with a misplaced enthusiasm. I'm constantly challenged to find the right words to speak at the right time to the right people. Yet it's worth it. My marriage, my children, my friendships, my extended family—all mean more to me than paying off $127K. I'm guessing your relationships matter more to you than your finances too.

I also beg you to fight the greed, envy, and judgment that might flood your soul like they did mine during our debt-slaying journey. The debt dragon doesn't just meddle in your bottom line; he seeks to destroy how you view others and yourself. It makes me sick to recount the number of times I coveted others' possessions, trips, experiences, shoes, and more. I worshiped someone else's journey, wanting to make it mine. I bowed to the created instead of the Creator. I longed for someone else's life. I invented excuses. Then I rationalized that it wasn't fair; surely they must be doing something "wrong." Now, I hear the words from the Gospel of Mark ringing through my ears: "What good is it for someone to gain the whole world, yet forfeit their soul?"[5]

We've all been given one journey. We've been given others who share that journey with us. Both are precious. When we exercise wisdom, both can help us slay the debt dragon. These words from the book of Romans served as a guide for our relationships and a high calling at the same time: "Love from the center of who you are; don't fake it. Run for dear life from evil; hold on for dear life to good. Be good friends who love deeply; practice playing second fiddle" (12:9-10). I'd love to tell you we made the wise choice in every single relationship—far from it. Time and time again, we returned to these words, remembering to love deeply with our words while still running for dear life from evil.

Debt-Slaying Strategies

✓ If you need to have a difficult conversation about your debt-slaying journey with a friend or family member, schedule a time to speak with them this week.

✓ Say thank you either by note or text this week to your family for areas where they support you. Express gratitude.

✓ Explore joining a Financial Peace University class or Crown Ministries Journey to Financial Freedom group.

✓ Intentionally cheer someone else on toward paying off debt.

Chapter 8

OF PRINCES AND PRINCESSES

Love the LORD your God with all your heart and with all your soul and with all your strength. These commandments that I give you today are to be on your hearts. Impress them on your children. Talk about them when you sit at home and when you walk along the road, when you lie down and when you get up. Tie them as symbols on your hands and bind them on your foreheads. Write them on the doorframes of your houses and on your gates.

DEUTERONOMY 6:5-9, NIV

FEAR FLOODED MY heart in the hours before I gave birth to the Princess Eldest. Quiet questions of self-doubt crept in and rocked my soul. *What if I don't love her? How can I love someone I have never even seen before? Will I be an awful mother?* Within seconds of hearing Anna's little cries and seeing her precious face (not to mention the locks of beautiful red hair upon her tiny head), the first two questions vanished. The third question? It lingers most days, especially when I fall short of my own expectations.

Yet of all the gifts that God has bestowed upon me, our two children are the greatest. I can never whisper "Thank You, Jesus" enough for them. They have taught me more about life, myself, and God's fierce love for His children than anyone else on the planet.

Indeed, children are a gift in a family. They bring laughter and joy. They can also bring tears and frustration. They hold up a mirror to our hearts, reflecting the best and worst parts of who we truly are. If we allow Him to, God will use our children to whittle away at the rough edges surrounding our souls, refining us as His sweet children. I'm certain we bring laughter and joy, tears and frustration to Him as well.[1]

You know what else children are? Expensive.

Having children costs money from the second they're conceived in your womb. Doctor's visits. Delivery costs. Car seats. Diapers. Clothes. Random contraptions like that little rubbery aspirator— which we always referred to as the "boogie sucker." And those are just some of the expenses that crop up during the first year of life.

The day we discovered we were pregnant with Anna, Brian and I made the rookie mistake of going to a baby superstore. We stood in sheer amazement at the number of gadgets, gizmos, and baby safety products we would *need* to purchase. What kind of parents would we be without all the modern conveniences to make sure our offspring was brilliant, safe, and felt loved?! (Note: If you are a first-time parent, *never* go to such a place on the day you discover you are expecting. You will avoid the heart attacks we both nearly had. When you do go to register for a baby shower, be sure to take an experienced parent with you. I promise that you can raise a brilliant, safe, and well-loved infant with about one percent of the stock at the baby superstore. People have been raising babies for millennia without high-end cloth diapers and fancy wipe warmers.)

Just after you've weathered the storms of baby gear, wellness checkups, diapers, formula or baby food, and preschool tuition, you begin to blaze the path toward elementary school. "Finally!" you exhale. "No more huge expenses!" Not so fast . . . enter braces, glasses, sports physicals, book fees, field trips, and shoes. (Do you know how many pairs of shoes your children are about to chuck through at a rapid pace?) Don't even get me started on the volume of food that teenagers consume or college tuition; let's just agree there are unanticipated and regular expenses that come along with every age.

CNN Money estimates that it will cost an average of $241,080 to raise a child born in 2012 through high school.[2] That is some serious coin, Lords and Ladies. Though that number may include some special activities and items we want our kids to enjoy, the majority of expenses are truly necessary. The wonderful, redemptive news is that special times like birthdays and back-to-school shopping trips do not need to break the bank. In addition, they provide the perfect platform to teach your children about the practice of budgeting and using money wisely.

Keep that in mind as you begin or persevere on your debt-slaying journey. Your belt tightening will provide your children with many real-life lessons that can help them avoid your financial missteps and blunders.

Beware the Parent Traps

Though you may know in your mind that getting your finances under control will help everyone in the long run, that doesn't necessarily make it easy to help your children understand why you're no longer able to do or buy what "everyone else" does.

Mommy and daddy guilt

When Brian and I contemplated our finances and realized that paying off debt would mean sacrifice, not just for us, but for our girls, too, I must admit that I had more than a twinge or two of guilt. Why should they have to pay for our stupidity? Why should they have to settle for less than what everyone else has? I firmly believe that questions like these are from the enemy, designed to paralyze us.

Yet those doubts emanate from a good place. We all love our children. We long to give them good gifts. I think it's a reflection of the Creator God within us, a mark of His image. After all, Matthew 7:9-11 says: "Which of you, if your son asks for bread, will give him a stone?

Or if he asks for a fish, will give him a snake? If you, then, though you are evil, know how to give good gifts to your children, how much more will your Father in heaven give good gifts to those who ask him!"[3]

When stretched too far, this very good gift of wanting to give our kids bread and fish rather than stones and snakes can twist our thinking and become a trap.[4] We actually begin to believe the lie that our children needn't suffer or reduce their lifestyles to "pay" for our financial missteps.

It's a bleak truth, but make no mistake: your children *will* pay for your money mistakes. Perhaps they won't have name brand jeans or the newest gaming system while you are paying off debt. Maybe your family won't be able to take that dream vacation. But consider the alternative. Let's say you forgo paying off debt and decide to do all of the above and then some. More than likely, your children will be saddled with the responsibility of taking out loans to pay for college or even caring for your financial needs when you are old and unable to work. It's a penny now, a pound later. Or said another way, it's a one-week vacation this year and years of financial burden for them when they have families of their own. Your children will end up in the very same place where you stand right now.

The truth is, however, that your children will not suffer while you are paying off debt—not really. Just consider the distribution of wealth on our planet. Rather than suffering, they will continue to enjoy many "luxuries" that children all over the world don't have. Things like shoes, a bed, electricity, and running water are gifts.

The monster under the bed

If your kids are young, you may assume you can shield them from your financial choices. After all, they can't possibly grasp the complexity of personal finance, right? *Wrong.*

Here's what I know about your children. They are incredibly intuitive and smart, and they come from a good gene pool. After all,

DEBT-SLAYING DUO

**BOB AND SUELLEN, 48 AND 46
PARENTS OF KATIE, 15; GLENN, 11** | **PAID OFF $98,607**

Each stage of raising children has its own unique financial challenges. Raising teenagers brings a host of expenses, as Bob and Suellen know firsthand. Their children are involved in many activities. But this family admits that the greatest hidden costs came from dining out frequently. "Because we were always running our teen somewhere, getting fast food had become a necessity of life. Having the discipline to prepare meals at home that could be eaten on the go was very challenging." In spite of this potential roadblock, the couple still paid off over $98K in twenty-one months.

Why slay the debt dragon?

Over the years, Bob and Suellen had cycled in and out of debt. However, as their children began to get older, the realities of saving for college and retirement set in for this pair. They knew that they wanted to provide a secure future for their family and that debt was preventing them from that dream. They had nothing saved. "We had lacked the discipline to change our habits. But middle age came, and we realized that we had to get serious about planning for our future."

What surprised them most about paying off debt?

Once they committed to eliminating debt, Bob and Suellen were shocked at how quickly the process actually went. Along the way they learned they could do without all sorts of things they'd once viewed as standard necessities.

What was most challenging?

As this duo began their debt-slaying journey, they struggled (as many married couples do) to decide where to begin cutting back. The more Bob and Suellen learned to work together, the less stress played a role in their marriage. Unforeseen surprise expenses cropped up a number of times as they pursued their goal, but through consistent communication and a shared dream, they learned how to handle those setbacks—together.

How did they celebrate?

In the two years before even embarking on their debt-slaying journey, the family had refused to finance a vacation on credit cards. They finally took a trip to celebrate being free from debt—their first "real vacation" in four years.

Their encouragement and advice for you

Bob and Suellen offer three essential pieces of wisdom. "First, no matter how bleak it seems, you *can* get out of debt if you stick to it, every single day. Second, set good ground rules up front as a couple so that making decisions along the way is easier during challenging times. Finally, bring God into your challenge and let Him lead, seek His wisdom, and listen intently to His guidance." Celebrating success was essential in this couple's story. "Go back and look at your successes to see how far you have already come. Look for new ways to pay off bills and be creative in your pursuit. If all else fails, look for one small victory you can obtain in the next thirty days, and make sure you accomplish it."

How has paying off debt changed their marriage?

With less stress in their lives, Bob and Suellen are better able to make wise financial decisions together. They feel better prepared to handle whatever life throws their way, commenting, "Paying off debt has brought a peace to our marriage so that we are focused on things other than money."

they have parents who read books and want to make good decisions about their finances. Don't fool yourself into thinking that your kids don't already know that you have problems with money. They do.

They have heard you admit to your spouse that you don't know how much is in your checking account. They have seen the glance of disapproval when you or your spouse made an outlandish purchase. They have heard the commonplace rejoinder of "We don't have enough money for that vacation (or appliance or restaurant or . . .)." They may even have heard you fight about your finances. No matter how quietly you think you are whispering, they hear you.

Kids are savvy. They pick up on way more than we think they do. They comprehend body language, innuendo, and hushed tones. Not only that, but kids are also ridiculously imaginative. The smallest of situations can become a full-blown nightmare in the mind of a child. I like to call this the "monster under the bed syndrome." Even a minor financial crisis is complete and utter destitution in the eyes of a child, if not explained properly.

Remember 2008, when the housing bubble burst? Nearly every single news report heralded problems on Wall Street and on Main Street. Anna was in kindergarten at the time. I remember her rushing to the picture window and staring out into the road with heightened alarm. Trembling, she wanted to know what sort of trouble was happening on

> Kids are savvy. They pick up on way more than we think they do.

Main Street. You see, we *live* on Main Street. A journalist's shocking metaphorical headline was a very real risk in her five-year-old imagination.

We stifled a giggle but took her concern very seriously. We didn't ignore her. We didn't laugh out loud (until later). Instead, we explained that there were very real problems in the nation's financial situation. Those problems stemmed from people borrowing money that they couldn't pay back. It was the perfect platform to teach her about our own freshly initiated journey away from accumulating debt. While we gave an elementary explanation of the current economic crisis, we also explained that she could be a part of the solution to our personal crisis.

Right on the Money

This is why it is incredibly important to regularly discuss your debt-slaying journey with your children from the very beginning. Of course, you want to use age-appropriate vocabulary and avoid scaring the living daylights out of them. But your discussion of finances should be a natural occurrence in your day-to-day life.

So much of what we do each day revolves around money. There are ample opportunities to open a discussion without having some sort of formal, sit-down talk that's uncomfortable for all of you. Let your conversation flow naturally and freely from what you are currently doing, and always look for an opportunity to provide an explanation.

Every time we go grocery shopping, I attempt to use the mundane task to teach both girls a number of lessons about money. On the ride to the store, I share with them our target budget for the trip. They help cross items off the list as we're shopping. For the past couple of years, Anna has taken over the duty of keeping a running total of our purchases on a calculator app. Not only does she help keep me on budget, but she has also begun to absorb knowledge of the prices of foods we regularly purchase. On some trips, I allow them each two dollars of the budget so they can choose a favorite food (within limits—no one is buying a big bag of candy) for the week. This little challenge helps both girls to own a part of our daily money experience.

I'll be honest. Sometimes I just want to go to the store by myself. I don't want to deal with requests for junk food or outside purchases.

However, a small investment of my time during the natural flow of our day is gradually teaching both of our girls how to handle money well and live within limits.

As much as you can, talk about biblical principles for finance while you sit at home—during meals, when helping with homework, while playing games, or while reading the Bible or other books together. Talk about money when "you walk along the road"—in the car, at the grocery store, while you're waiting at the doctor's office, before guitar lessons or soccer practice. Don't forget to talk about the importance of contentment, gratitude, and an abundant life "when you lie down and when you get up."[5]

Recognize that your child may have some interesting theories about where money comes from and how it is used. No matter how much we wish it were so, we need to dispel our kids' mistaken impression that cash is something you can just "get" anytime you pull up to the ATM. It's not a magical money contraption or carnival game. Nor does having the money in savings mean you buy whatever you want whenever you want it. To help them better understand the scope of your family's responsibilities, you may want to introduce a basic financial vocabulary into your household. Explain words like *mortgage*, *debt*, and *checking account* and the difference between debit and credit. Begin at square one, assuming they know little or nothing about how money should be handled.

When we embarked on our own debt-slaying adventure, we were very up front with our girls. I guess I should say "girl" because the Princess Youngest was an infant and probably didn't understand what we were saying. The Princess Eldest was five years old and completely capable of comprehending the basics. We explained that we were going to pay off debt and that our lifestyle would be greatly reduced. That meant we wouldn't be eating out at restaurants or buying toys "just because." We would need to sacrifice as an entire family. We set family goals for paying off debt.

Some Days
August 2011 blog post

Some days,
  it feels like this is such a long and lonely battle
  that it doesn't really matter why we do what we do,
  like we're stuck on an enormous Ferris wheel–sized hamster
    wheel.

Some days,
  it seems like everyone else is having so much fun
  going on big vacations (again),
  eating at fancy restaurants (again),
  at the movie theater (again),
  going to a fun concert (again),
  while we eat peanut butter and jelly and read books from the
    library at home on the couch.

Some days,
  I get jealous of new laptops, pretty clothes, well-decorated
    homes, and iPhones.
  I envy minivans, date nights where you hire a babysitter, and
    nice towels.
  I long for Starbucks purchased without a gift card, new run-
    ning shoes, and pedicures.

Some days,
  I snuggle in bed with the Princesses under a well-worn and
    torn blanket (and I am content).
  I spend time munching on homemade popcorn and watching
    a movie on our hand-me-down TV with the King of Free
    (and I am content).
  I receive encouragement on my not very smartphone via text
    or a call from a friend (and I am content).
  I feast on zucchini grown in our garden (and I am content).
  I play in our homemade sprinkler with the Princesses and the
    King of Free (and I am content).

> I realize how many adventures we've gone on and how many
> blessings we've received since we began our journey (and
> I am content).
> I count the days of our battle and number the amounts we
> have paid since the very beginning—and I am content and
> overwhelmed by God's grace, blessing, and goodness.
> $105,936.48 since April 2008. Nine . . . more . . . months.
> We CAN do this. You can too.
>
> I've learned by now to be quite content whatever my cir-
> cumstances. I'm just as happy with little as with much, with
> much as with little. I've found the recipe for being happy
> whether full or hungry, hands full or hands empty. Whatever
> I have, wherever I am, I can make it through anything in the
> One who makes me who I am. (Philippians 4:11-13)

I remember throwing a big boohoo pity party for myself not long after that. Maybe it was mommy guilt; maybe I was using my girls as an excuse to feel sorry for myself. But I remember wallowing in my own filth and thinking, *We're never ever going to have fun anymore. We won't be able to go to the children's museum. We won't be able to go to the zoo. We won't go to art museums. We won't be able to do all of those fun things that enrich the lives of families and boost the intelligence of children.*

I was sure my children were doomed to be dolts, living in a color-less, no-fun world. These sentiments must have brought a chuckle from the lips of the Divine. For a mere six months later, after plenty of faithful daily sacrifice and frugal living, I found myself in the offices of the nearest major metropolitan convention and visitor's association. After interviewing me, they told me they wanted to pay me to write about taking my family on really awesome adventures throughout the city.[6] I jumped at the opportunity and took the job. If not for the relationships I developed while blogging about our debt-slaying journey, we would have missed the opportunity to do some of the oddest and most fun activities together. From sitting front row at an NBA game to meeting Jared Fogle from Subway to flying in a World War II plane upside down over Lake Michigan, I quickly discovered my pity party had been unwarranted.[7]

One of our first big milestones would be paying off the $16,500 balance on one of our credit cards. When we had paid off most of the balance, we decided that once we eliminated it completely, we would celebrate by going to a nearby indoor water park for the weekend. Not long afterward, the Princess Eldest, who was then in second grade, went with me to Target. While we were there, something caught her eye. (It was so radically important that neither of us can remember what it was now.) I do remember her saying, "I really would like to have that, but I'd much rather go to Great Wolf Lodge." It was one of those parenting "*Yes!*" moments, complete with the fist pump. For a year and a half I'd been explaining and reminding and reinforcing the lessons of delayed gratification and sacrifice, all to reach a greater goal. In that moment, I knew my daughter's heart had changed and a ray of light had broken through.

If you explain your current situation in a positive way and with an attitude of "and we need your help," more than likely your children will be ready to jump into the journey with you. No, they're not always going to understand why you can't dine out or buy that toy or go on vacation or give them a cell phone or why you aren't like everyone else. However, your excitement and joy for your journey can be contagious.

On the contrary, if your attitude about your current financial situation stinks, your child will be a mirror image of you. If you are throwing a pity party, don't be surprised when they bring the "noise-makers" and join in the festivities. Your children are often a reflection of your current state of being. Sometimes, they're just cray cray because they are children. But it's always good to ask if perhaps some of the biggest challenges with your children are due to the inclination of your own heart. (Man, I hate it when I write a sentence that causes me to pause and acknowledge my own mistakes. Ouch.)

You might not get the opportunity to see your life flash before your eyes as you're flying upside down in a 1940s-era plane, but I am convinced that once you commit to following God's guidelines for giving, saving, and spending money, you will have many opportunities to delight in ways that He provides for even your smallest and most inconsequential needs. You will begin to look for His loving-kindness in an amazing, wildly adventurous family treasure hunt. Yes, there will be sacrifice, but it doesn't have to be suffering unless you term it so.

My friends Bob and Suellen saw God draw their family closer during their debt-slaying journey too. With their daughter heading off to college in just a couple of years, their number of potential family vacations seemed to be vanishing before their very eyes. Yet they knew they wanted to persist in their journey. Instead of diminishing their progress, or worse, accruing more debt, their family decided to have a fun and much more cost-effective "staycation." For a week solid, they looked for exciting and low-cost activities in their own backyard. From hiking at a beautiful park (free!) to a minor league baseball game (made much more affordable by great coupons), this family became tourists in their own city every day of the week. They saved money on hotel costs and boarding the dog by staying at home and gained the experience of visiting places they might have missed otherwise. At the end of the week everyone agreed that it was the very best vacation they had ever taken. What could have easily turned into a pity party—"We *never* get to vacation now that we're paying off debt"—was transformed into a unique experience that knit this sweet family closer together.

"I don't think we would have ever planned a vacation like that if we hadn't been trying to pay off debt," Suellen said to me. They would have missed both the staycation adventure and the opportunity to deepen their relationships.

But What about Birthdays?

I love nothing more than a celebration—especially birthdays. When mine comes around, the King of Free blesses me with *seven* whole days to celebrate. He calls it "the seven days of Cherie." I get a gift each day. #Swoon. I know what you are thinking. *I thought you people were frugal! How frugal is it to give* seven *birthday gifts?* Mind you, while the gifts are wonderful and filled with much thought, they rarely cost a lot. In fact, the King of Free has been known to clean out a closet as a "gift."

The year he bought me two Matchbox cars, it meant more to me than diamonds. For months, I had eyeballed the stair railing at our apartment complex. I finally told Brian that it looked like the perfect width for a Matchbox car racetrack. I shrieked with joy when I opened the package and found the toy cars. Then we sat on the stairs for what felt like hours as I rolled those little boogers down the rail and watched them *smack!* into the wall over and over again. (I'm sure the neighbors thought it was great.)

Bottom line, gifts don't have to cost a lot to bring great joy or convey meaning. So before you consider launching a crowd-sourcing campaign to buy our girls all the gifts they missed out on while we were paying off our debt, I can assure you that we did take care of all their needs and even blessed them with gifts. We were, however, more deliberate about distinguishing between wants and needs.

Of course, that seems to go against current trends. Imagine exquisite and complicated themes, expensive favors, and mouthwatering catered food. No, I'm not talking about one of this summer's hottest premiere parties or even a grand wedding. Spend three minutes on Pinterest and you'll quickly realize that such things are now featured at your average suburban three-year-old's birthday party. People, it's getting a little ridiculous out there. But the good news is that you can stop the madness. The great over-the-top birthday fiasco can stop with *you*. Birthdays can be special without a huge price tag attached.

Here are a few of my favorite ways of saving money while celebrating our daughters' birthdays.

Limit the number of friend fiestas. Choose to limit the number of "friend" birthday parties that you allow your children to have. We celebrate the "big" birthdays—one, five, ten, and eventually sixteen with friends; however, in the off years we celebrate only with our families or a few close family friends. Limiting the number of parties you throw cuts down on expense as well as the ugly—too much birthday monster (haven't you read that Berenstain Bears book?[8]). Lest you think that your child will suffer incredible emotional and mental anguish from this practice, the Princess Eldest (now eleven) can barely remember her fifth birthday party. We invited a crowd of her little friends to one of those germy bounce house places. We played video games. Anna opened presents. She only "remembers" the details when we show her pictures or remind her of them.

Choose fancy napkins, plain plates. There's no need to buy every single matching party item. Remember that the majority of those cute party decorations will be in the trash by the end of your prince's or princess's special day. Let your child choose his or her favorite character or theme-based napkin, and then get plain or generic coordinating plates and cups. Better yet, pick up a number of reusable items (yay for being green and saving greenbacks!) that will match a wide array of themes. Our collection of red bowls, cups, baskets, and more matches almost any theme and holiday (think Valentine's Day, Memorial Day, the Fourth of July, Christmas).

Hire inexpensive (or free) teens. Still feel like you need an entertainment element to your party? Instead of hiring a scary and expensive clown, consider hiring your babysitter or a local high school athlete to keep the kids occupied. From baseball players to cheerleaders, from aspiring artists to garage bands, many high schoolers in your community are wildly talented and also wildly unemployed. See if you know someone who fits your theme and then invite him or her to come and entertain. Whether the teen is good with pets or a paintbrush, two things are for sure: he or she is cooler than you are and hungry for work.

Keep it simple. I'll call it the KIS principle because I don't think you're stupid. One Google search or Pinterest inquiry will prove that birthday parties are perhaps a little OOC (out of control; I'm all over the acronyms in this tip). Ask your kiddo if he or she *really* wants a big party. You may be surprised to discover that it's not what your child wants, even if you do. You might be able to take one friend to a children's museum, movie, or even a theme park for less than what you'd spend on a party. Consider all the options before launching into big-party mode.

Delegate the budgeting. For her ninth birthday, the Princess Eldest managed the birthday budget for her family party. She kept track of the money and planned the menu. She bought the decorations and cake from the cash budget we gave to her to manage. It was a fabulous learning experience and helped her sort through what was really important and what she could skip. The birthday party theme was "Fiesta!" and included a taco bar and a piñata filled with candy. Because she took ownership, Anna can recount more details about this party than I remember.

Think outside the cake. No matter what your Netflix queue tries to tell you, parties don't require the *Cake Boss*, *Cupcake Wars*, or the bakers from *DC Cupcakes*. Seriously, while decorating them can make them look cool, cakes are designed to be *eaten*. As long as it doesn't end up being featured on the *Cake Wrecks* blog, your kid is going to love it. Birthday milkshakes, a sundae bar, make-your-own strawberry shortcake, or even pancakes may get the job done just as well, if not better. Once again, *ask your child*. Be prepared to do something crazy, though, as you never know what he or she might really want.

Showing your child how much you love him or her through a fancy party each year is *not* worth going into debt. Having a slamming sixth birthday party will not pay for your child's college education. Think before you spend, and most of all, remember that spending time with—not money on—your children is the best way to show them how much you love them!

The Grinch Who Stole Christmas

True story: The King of Free and I did not give each other Christmas gifts for four years while we were paying off debt. We also gave up Mother's Day, Father's Day, and anniversary gifts. He requested that I not give him anything for his birthday. I'd like to think this was a much bigger sacrifice for me than it was for him. I *love* gifts. I love to receive them. I love to painstakingly choose gifts. I love to wrap gifts. I love to noodle on what will best celebrate someone's passions and loves and then turn that into a gift. I love scheduled gifts. I love spontaneous gifts. I love gifts! . . . confetti! . . . ribbons! . . . presents!

At first, it was extremely difficult for me to let go of the notion of gifts not being a part of our Christmas tradition. When we received Christmas or birthday gifts of money from our family or friends, they went straight onto the debt snowball or were used to purchase items the girls needed. We were practical to the *n*th degree. True confession: At first it made me a little sad. But as we gained more success,

I realized that a new trinket was not worth as much to me as the freedom we would one day gain. Plus, speaking from experience, gifts that you give when you're debt-free are way more awesome because they come with more thought, more expendable cash, and less guilt. The first Christmas after we paid off our last debt, we did give each other gifts and it was fun. But the second Christmas, we opted to just give each other stockings with small gifts. We are simple people.

As is often true in life, the rules we legislate for adults aren't the same as the ones we impose on children. Our girls received Christmas presents even when the King of Free and I were not exchanging them ourselves. But the tradition in our home has always looked a little bit different from that in many households. We knew early on that we wanted to be careful to ensure that our kids didn't turn into "present crack" addicts at Christmas time. We didn't want them tearing through a package without even looking at what they'd received, all the while looking for the next brightly bowed box to rip up. In that euphoric environment, all you'd have to do is add some flashing lights and electronic dance music and they'd be at a rave.

While gifts are a part of our Christmas experience, we try to keep the chaos and over-"stuffing" (referring to the process of collecting of stuff, not the delicious dish) to a minimum. Here are a few guidelines we followed while slaying the debt dragon and continue to follow today.

Give three gifts. By the grace of God and through the wisdom of friends further down the road of parenting, we instituted this from the Princess Eldest's first Christmas. So this practice was in place long before we began our debt-slaying journey. We give our girls one larger toy or electronic device. It might be costly, it might not, but it is wowie-zowie, something they have been dreaming of with child-like wonder. The second gift is an article of clothing, which probably means more to my tween than it does to my kindergartener. Still, it's a good idea to help your children realize that a coat is a gift, a *very* good gift. Children all over the world don't have coats, let alone beautiful blue coats with ruffles. It might be a dress or a leotard or a scarf or even a pair of new shoes that your child needs. Whatever it is, it's important to convey that a met need is also a blessing and can be a gift too. The third gift the Princesses receive is a book. Reading is a joy and a treasure in our home.

The three gifts represent the three treasures given to Jesus by the magi. I also like this tradition because it helps me to focus in on one item that my girls would *love* and avoid giving into the yearly temptation of picking up "just one more thing!" We also sidestep the trap of purchasing four or five $10 to $20 toys, many of which I would have to clean up from the floor during the next calendar year.

Fill stockings with a mix of necessities and small fun items. I am *that* mom. I will give one of my daughters a toothbrush for Christmas and expect her to like it—nay, *love* it. From fun body wash to nail polish to food, I might splurge on an item that costs a wee bit more or has a character on it, but practicality is still a blessing.[9]

I'm not a complete killjoy, however. Occasionally, I'll use reward points to pick up a free movie, small stuffed animal, candy, costume jewelry, or other small, fun items. I also shy away from the stocking stuffer area of local superstores or discount stores since most of the seasonal items there will end up being thrown away the week or two after Christmas. I don't know too many kids who want to color with reindeer markers on December 28 or use Santa lip gloss in January. When I'm debating on whether or not to make a purchase, I hold an item up and imagine stepping on it in the middle of the night three months from now. Again, you should spend just a wee bit more on something that will last longer rather than loading up on cheap, disposable gifts.

Provide guided gift lists to the grandparents. The Queen and King's Mums ask for them, and I'm happy to supply. If at all possible, our immediate and extended families coordinate gifts that can be played with together. For example, one family gives a gaming system; the other purchases games. Or play food is purchased to go along with a kitchen set. The grandparents still have the ability to choose something within a range of both prices and our princesses' wishes, but it helps all of us to be happier when the gifts are unwrapped.

Give gifts of presence. Baking cookies, reading books, watching holiday movies, decorating, going out and about shopping, visiting friends and family, and more can be the greatest gifts of all. When you reflect on your best Christmas ever, usually your memories have to do with people, *not* things. Go ahead. Close your eyes and allow yourself to be transported to a Christmas of your past. What do you smell? What do you hear? Who do you see? What are you doing? I had one awesome Christmas where I received a faux–rabbit fur coat, mini cowgirl boots, and blue Barbie eye shadow (the 80s were a rough decade). By and large, I can't remember what I received as a child on other years, though. (Oh, I almost forgot the scary Ronald McDonald doll I wanted so badly. Yikes.) What about you? More than likely, you long for the presence of someone who is no longer on the earth or wish to recapture the fun things you did way more than you wish you had a Cabbage Patch doll again.

Practice generosity. Even while we were paying off debt, we were intentional about giving a gift to someone else. Some years we put together baskets of food for a local community stretched to its limits. Some years we chose a card from a Prison Fellowship's Angel Tree program. Some years we gave money to a charity. Every Christmas, we carol at a local nursing home with our community group. Celebrating Jesus' birth should have nothing to do with us and everything to do with showing up in the lives of others to surprise them with His very good news and great glad tidings.

This *can* be a bit tricky, though. There are so many charities and very good things that tug at our hearts during the Christmas season. You can't give to everyone. Set a budget for generosity. (This includes baking cookies for your neighbors, because butter and flour aren't free.) Then stick with it.

Bottom line, good gifts are *great* things. Again, I firmly believe that gift giving is a beautiful reflection of the image of God within us all. God gives good gifts to His children. We're driven to do the same. That being said, there are limits. Your children don't want your gifts. They want you. Give them a gift of great value at Christmas. Keep it simple.

Back-to-School Budgeting

Every era of parenting brings with it a significant price tag. Not long after we give that huge sigh of relief because we no longer have to pay for diapers every stinking (literally) week, most parents are hit with a new reality: back-to-school shopping. The National Retail Federation said the average family spent $634.78 in 2013 on supplies, apparel, shoes, and electronics as students prepared to head back to school.[10] Obviously, the actual total will depend on the number and grade levels of your kids, but we've found that with intentionality there are some ways to really save in this area.

As with birthday celebrations, back-to-school purchases provide a great platform to teach kids about budgeting and saving money. Maybe the following suggestions will spark some ideas to maximize your dollars and the learning experience.

Check the list. Be sure to get copies of your children's supply list for their specific classrooms. Many schools place these lists on their websites well before school begins; they might even have been included with registration materials sent out the previous spring. There is nothing worse than purchasing the wrong brand of a product. Know what you need before you ever hit the aisles.

Take an inventory. Once you have the supply list, go on a treasure hunt in your own house. Beginning with a mind-set of wealth rather than poverty can actually curb your spending. I guarantee many of the things you need are already in your possession. Block off an afternoon to inventory the items—clothing and supplies—that you already have. I'm not suggesting you send your kids back to school with broken pencils and worn-down crayons; however, items like backpacks, lunchboxes, rulers, scissors, and flash drives can be used for more than one school year.

Next, clean out your kids' closets and drawers. Have them try on clothes to see what fits. Most important, as you determine what you need, write it down. This will keep you from overspending. Use the school's supply list and your written inventory for clothes and supplies to create your own back-to-school hit list.

Use cash. You've already heard me say it multiple times, but it bears repeating: you will *always* spend less if you use cash rather than plastic, even if it's a debit card. Cash provides a boundary around your budget; it's a hedge that ensures you spend exactly what you intend and not a penny more. Plus, it's a great lesson for the kids to hear you say, "We only have enough cash for this" or "We can buy one of these or two of those." If your children are old enough, allow them to be the keeper of the cash. Physically holding the money will empower them with responsibility while also reinforcing limits. Also, it makes the cash the bad guy instead of you. When the cash is gone, you are finished shopping.

Allow your child to fail. A mantra of Andy Stanley's that we often repeat is "Don't bail, let them fail."[11] More than likely, if you do allow your children to actively participate in the back-to-school budgeting and spending, they will make mistakes. As parents, there's a driving force within us to swoop in, save our children from all harm, and correct their mistakes *before* they even make them. This is the perfect time to pause and provide guidance but allow your children to completely and utterly mess up. You'll have a well-timed opportunity to talk about what happens when we purchase too many pencils but not enough socks. Best of all, you can extend grace to your child and teach eternal lessons too. While you don't want to make your kid wear shirts with holes to school, if you truly want to allow your children to learn about finances, then allow them to make mistakes. We all learn our best lessons in life from "oops" moments.

> If you truly want to allow your children to learn about finances, then allow them to make mistakes. We all learn our best lessons in life from "oops" moments.

Write down every penny you spend. This tip is really to help you the following academic year. Record every back-to-school expense down to the penny—from book fees to PTO, from gym suits to new shoes, from school supplies to classroom extras. If you keep good records now, you won't have to choose a pie-in-the-sky number when you set your budget for next year. It's also helpful to look at the textbook fees for your children's grade level next year to get a good estimate of what you will be spending then.

When you can, buy extras. If your cash budget allows, purchase extra school supplies now to create a small stockpile that you can use the rest of the year. Your child will need new markers. She will rip up a folder. Notebook paper will run out. There is no better time of year to purchase school supplies since many retailers offer them at rock-bottom prices in the late summer and early fall. Poster board and other office supplies also tend to be a bit cheaper just before school starts. Not only will you save money by picking them up now, you won't need to worry about having to head out late some night when your child suddenly remembers he or she needs something for a special project the next day.

Take a pass on most fund-raisers. Want to know where I still struggle with mommy guilt? Fund-raisers. Inevitably, the order forms start coming home during the first few weeks of school. I want to buy every roll of wrapping paper, order every pie, purchase every bar of candy and box of cookies I can. While we were paying off debt, we did the absolute minimum in this area. We ordered one item from our own children and nothing from anyone else. You simply cannot order from every catalog from every kid who rings your doorbell and bats his or her eyes at you. *Oh those sweet little eyes!* Don't let your mommy guilt blind you to the truth that this fund-raiser is not in your budget. Someday when you're debt-free, a kid down the street may hit the jackpot when you spend $200 on an order of stuff you probably don't need. But for now, go look in the mirror, practice your sad eyes, and say a polite "no" over and over again until you're ready for the little salespeople to ~~harass~~ pitch to you.

Enact a co-pay system. My mommy guilt weakness for fund-raisers extends to yearbooks, school T-shirts, lollipops during lunch hour, book orders, and class photos. Midway through our debt-slaying journey, I began offering co-pays for items like these to my girls. If they wanted an "extra" like a yearbook, they needed to use some of their own funds to purchase it. I usually cover at least half of the cost of such items; however, the girls still "feel" the expense.

I'll never forget the time the Princess Eldest wanted to order a class picture. As we debated the necessity of that purchase, I asked where last year's photo was. When she couldn't come up with an answer, I pulled it from the kitchen countertop, where it was still neatly stored in the wrapper from the previous academic year. All of a sudden, it didn't seem like such an urgent need to her. Again, you cannot purchase every item your school, PTO, team, or troop is selling. Such purchases fall into a category that is much less important than the pursuit of paying off debt. Knowing this is simple. Practicing it isn't always easy.

Allowances, Loans, Commerce, and Other Things

For someone so crazy about teaching kids about money, it might come as a shock to learn that I'm not a fan of allowances. My guess is no one pays you just to wake up each day, right? Pennies don't rain from heaven so you can pay your mortgage. Food doesn't magically appear on the dinner table just because you are an awesome human being. Money comes from work. Money accumulates when we save it. Money loses its power over us when we give. Money earned is actually fun to spend. These are priceless lessons for us to learn, right along with our children.

> Money comes from work. Money accumulates when we save it. Money loses its power over us when we give. Money earned is actually fun to spend. These are priceless lessons for us to learn, right along with our children.

No worries—if you have decided to give your child an allowance, I have no plans to come to your house to rip it out of your son's or daughter's tiny hands. If you are overseeing the process, there are plenty of ways to teach your little ones about money through allowance. However, it is not a system we adopted. Here's why.

There are certain things our girls do to get to live in the Lowe household. They must keep relative order in their rooms. (I'm fairly lenient. Remember, no neat as a pin here.) They must be kind to each other. They must pick up their clothes and even the clothes of others when asked. They must empty the dishwasher if they are old enough to reach the cabinets. They must do their homework. They must listen to their parents. They must clear their dishes from the dinner table. For all of the above and a few more "you musts" I'm forgetting, they are awarded a room in which to keep all of their awesome stuff, beds to sleep in, three square meals a day, and their own personal taxi service that takes them to and from daily activities.

These daily tasks are expectations for being in our family. While we wouldn't boot the girls to the curb for not doing them, we also will not pay them for being a part of our family. We agreed on this philosophy long before our children made their way onto the planet. Living as a family requires sacrifice for us all. Sacrifice and love are not compensated monetarily in our home.

Even so, there *are* jobs our little princesses can do to make money. Usually said jobs are ones that are less than pleasant and might require some extra effort. We may also compensate the girls for stellar grades—with cash, goods, or perhaps dinner out. Our girls began this system of employment around the age of three by removing the towels from the dryer.

The cash compensation is probably meager in comparison to most households. We pay by the dime or even by the penny sometimes. Payday is based on when they do work, not necessarily a set day of the week. When they are paid, they are expected to place 10 percent of their earnings into their "Give" bank or envelope. Another 10 percent is deposited into their savings. The rest can go into their "Spend" bank or wallet. Even monetary gifts received from their grandparents (because *they do* pay the girls to be cute from time to time) must be divided into the above categories. Once again, there are printable cash budget envelopes on QueenOfFree.net just for you. The "kid" versions have cute pictures on the front and quotes on the back to discuss as a family.

Anna and Zoe get to choose what they do with their "Spend" money. If they lose their spend money in the store, it is not replaced. If they forget to bring it with them, we do not loan them money. Even if they *only* need one more dollar, they have to wait until they have saved one more dollar.

Our intention is not to make life more difficult for them but to prepare them to handle money themselves one day. As part of that training, we also offer plenty of incentives and coaching. We will:

- **Help our kids score the best deal on their purchase.** This includes scouring for coupons for everything from gum to American Girl clothes and comparing prices offered by stores *before* we leave the house. Even if it takes extra time from our day, we will guide them through this process and teach them how to effectively bargain and make the most of their money.

- **Offer a matching program.** If they have a long-term savings goal, like a laptop or even a car, we will match their funds up to a set amount. By age eleven, Princess Eldest had already drafted and gotten us to sign an agreement that outlines how much we will match for the purchase of her first car.

- **Provide for their needs.** We don't ask our girls to buy their own underwear or cough up a contribution for the weekly food allowance. The items we deem necessities will be covered, no questions asked and no complaints given. Of course, Reese's Peanut Butter Cups are not needs. Neither are potato chips. Neither is that really cute pair of jeans when there are already four pairs in the drawer. A toy is never considered a need.

- **Assist in setting long-term and short-term savings goals.** Saving indefinitely without a goal in mind will either create indifference or make money into an idol. Setting both short-term and long-term savings goals can help avoid both extremes. You can do this even with the youngest of children. Sometimes a desire rises while we're in the store, and I make note that Anna or Zoe could begin saving for that item. I won't lie; sometimes I "plant" a goal in one of the girl's heads to save for a book or another item I think might benefit their development. More than once, we have printed out pictures of a product and taped them to a bank to focus on a savings goal. Even if it's a stuffed animal or a video game, a visual reminder will keep a child zeroed in on their goals. (Side note: it works for adults, too.)

The Greatest Family Adventure

The psalmist reminds us, "Children are a gift from the LORD; they are a reward from him" (Psalm 127:3, NLT).

In the day in, day out stuff of life, we can lose sight of the big picture. Parenting children is a wearisome endeavor, not for the weak in heart, body, and spirit. Often, instead of seeing living presents, we see little monsters who are always wanting something else from us . . . another snack . . . another toy . . . another story . . . another drink before bed . . . another treat . . . another ride . . . another permission slip . . . another . . .

Their little hands smudge the glass you just cleaned. Their little cries keep you from sleeping at night. Their little diapers fill. Then they fill again. Their little attitudes sometimes smell like their little diapers. Their little mouths repeat words that make you cringe. We forget that our children are actually these amazing little gifts, given straight from the hand of God.

On your weariest and hairiest of child-rearing days, take a deep breath and a brief step back. Realize that those little beings were not placed in your life to make your existence miserable. They are a reward. Beyond that, those little faces, little hands, and little feet will someday be much more than requesters of "another." Raising your children is of eternal value and makes a huge difference in our world. Your children aren't merely children; they are future doctors, authors, teachers, pastors, nonprofit workers, chefs, artists, lawyers, journalists, and best of all, the future moms and dads who will parent your grandchildren. The difference they make doesn't have to begin in the future either. It begins today.

While a high calling and certainly a challenge, parenting enables you to partner with God in the formation of eternal souls. He has plans to give your children hope and a future.[12] Allow Him to lead even the youngest members of your family on the great adventure of learning to trust Him to provide for your needs (and even some of your wants) while you take on debt. One day, the verses they memorize in Sunday school may slip their minds. They may forget the order of the books of the Bible. Nothing, however, will ever erase the memories of the times that their very personal God provided for their family as they chose to follow His plan for their finances.

Debt-Slaying Strategies

✓ Sit down with your children to discuss your current financial situation. Be sure that all electronic devices are powered down and you're not pinched for time. Let them ask questions, and then be sure to answer them.

✓ Help your children set goals for your family. Whether planning a milestone celebration or coloring in a giant thermometer to track how much debt has been paid off, be intentional about involving them in your debt-slaying journey.

✓ Set up a chore chart and outline ways your child can earn money. Be sure to set an agreed-upon pay scale and decide when payday will be.

✓ Assist your child in choosing both short-term and long-term savings goals. Be sure the goals are realistic for their income. Print out pictures of the goals and place them on a bank or envelope.

✓ Print out the Give, Save, and Spend kids' cash envelopes from QueenOfFree.net.

Chapter 9

JOY FOR THE JOURNEY: A BENEDICTION

Eucharisteo—thanksgiving—always precedes the miracle.
ANN VOSKAMP

I ARRIVED HOME to find a big white trash bag slumped on my front step—filled with hand-me-downs for the Princess Youngest, I assumed. A new friend I barely knew had mentioned she was going to drop a few things off at our home. Her Facebook message mentioned there were some items she had cleaned out of her own closet too.

We were so close to the end of our debt-slaying journey, I could taste it. Yet the final payment loomed off in what seemed to be the untouchable future. We had paid off over $125K in debt. I knew it was a miracle to have come this far. But in the last two months, I had struggled with discouragement, bitterness, and even disbelief that we would ever truly slay the debt dragon. Looking back, it seems absolutely ridiculous, but in the midst of the situation, my feelings were very real. In some ways, the last sixty days were more difficult than the previous 1,396.

I tore into the bag and began sorting through what I thought would fit our daughter and what was too big. When someone gives your child hand-me-downs, it's a blessing. When someone gives *you* hand-me-downs, it can feel insulting. However, my clothes were absolutely shabby by the end of our journey. It was rare that I purchased anything for myself. I could get by with yoga pants and stained T-shirts most days, even though they were beginning to wear thin. I longed to buy just a new item or two for the spring season—something that didn't have holes in it.

My fingers ran over the clothing she had included for me—beautiful brand-name items with the tags still attached, in styles and colors I loved. Each fit perfectly. Tears filled my eyes as I realized God was saying, "I'm still here. I still care about you. Even in the smallest of things, in the simplest of ways, I provide." My thoughts rushed headlong to Jesus' words to His disciples in Matthew 6:28-30:

> Why worry about your clothing? Look at the lilies of the field and how they grow. They don't work or make their clothing, yet Solomon in all his glory was not dressed as beautifully as they are. And if God cares so wonderfully for wildflowers that are here today and thrown into the fire tomorrow, he will certainly care for you. Why do you have so little faith? (NLT)

Certainly, my faith had grown during our four-year journey, and yet I had once again fallen into the trap of thinking that God didn't care about the small details of my life. In His grand generosity, He hadn't shamed me or condemned me for my lack of faith. Instead, God had shown up inside of a bulging trash bag of hand-me-downs. Someone else's cast-off clothing displayed His glory in the quietest of ways.

As I sat on the floor of my bedroom, I wept and whispered words of choked-up gratitude. I'm not sure if my friend had any idea how deeply my soul had been struggling with lack—of clothes, of faith, of encouragement. Perhaps she was thankful to lighten her own load and clear away clutter. Maybe God had nudged her that day and she had no idea why. She's never dropped off a bag of hand-me-downs at our house again. Yet her simple act of obedience did more than she'll probably ever know.

Slaying the debt dragon brings wearisome fatigue. You wonder if the battle will ever end. Your heart yearns for freedom while your finances remain indefinitely chained. Open your eyes to see where God wants to remind you that He cares for the smallest of details. He tends to the tiniest of needs. Even when your faith is small, His love is enormous.

> **Even when your faith is small, God's love is enormous.**

As I carted the contents of the white trash bag to the laundry room, I realized that God had shown up and my physical needs had been met that day. The deep longing of my heart to draw closer to the Creator had been eased too.

We're Having a Party and *You're All* Invited

While working toward any worthwhile, soul-stretching goal, our emotions inevitably oscillate between incredible highs and lows. Although I battled discouragement—along with debt—on some days, at other times I soared on the knowledge that my family was on the path toward true freedom.

About two years into our journey, I was sharing our story with a MOPS group[1] on a rainy Wednesday morning when I impulsively invited this group of strangers to my house for a party once our family had paid off all our debt.

Inviting thirty women I didn't really know to a party that wasn't even on my calendar to celebrate a goal I hadn't yet reached *might not* have been my best social move ever. I'm sure Emily Post would have disapproved of my timing.

But in the day in, day out struggles to pay off over $127K, Brian and I needed something to fix our eyes upon. We needed a goal out in the distance, something we could see faintly, as if through the fog. We needed hope to supply joy for the downright drudgery that telling ourselves no over and over again could bring. So we decided to throw a debt-free party after the final installment on our Sallie Mae loan was paid.

Feasts, parties, and banquets are sprinkled throughout the Bible. From the wedding where Jesus turned water into wine to the giant "camping party" that was the Feast of Tabernacles, our God delights in throwing a smashing party with a purpose. He shows up at the table, ready to delight with us. How amazing is that? Not only does He long for a relationship with His people, He desires for us to join in the divine extravaganza that He's throwing, all expenses paid. Heaven itself is described as a banquet feast. And in spite of my fundamentalist upbringing, I just *know* there will be dancing in heaven.

Our inspiration for throwing a debt-free party came from a parable that Jesus told in Luke 15:8-10:

> Suppose a woman has ten silver coins and loses one. Doesn't she light a lamp, sweep the house and search carefully until she finds it? And when she finds it, she calls her friends and neighbors together and says, "Rejoice with me; I have found my lost coin." In the same way, I tell you, there is rejoicing in the presence of the angels of God over one sinner who repents. (NIV)

Deep in our hearts, Brian and I longed to celebrate what we had found. What had been lost for us hadn't necessarily been money, even though God helped us "find" $127K to pay off our debt over four years. What we had lost was so much more.

We had lost a sense of contentment.
We had lost a dependence on God to supply all of our needs.
We had lost the bigger picture of the adventure God wanted to
    take us on through our story.

Living day to day, paying bill after bill, our lives had been locked into a boring status quo existence. There was little space for God's wonder, little room to notice His quest to free our souls. We were too busy looking at our feet to cast our glance upward and even acknowledge His daily glorious presence. We would still be in that same place, chained and tethered by debt, without His grace.

On the white bookshelf of the cotton-candy-pink bedroom of the Princess Youngest is a children's book I have read over and over again to both our girls. *It's Not Funny, I've Lost My Money!* retells this very parable in a sing-song form. The cartoon widow searches all through her home, retraces her steps from the day before, and employs a number of other search tactics. We giggle each time she exclaims, "It's not funny, I've lost my money!" Finally the widow lights a lamp, sweeps with all her might, and spies a tiny glimmer from the coin in the corner of her home. Overwhelmed with gratitude, she calls together *everyone* she knows and throws the party of the century.[2]

Certainly we identified with both the coin and the widow at different points in our journey. As we considered God's work in our lives before our debt-slaying journey began, we saw that He had never stopped searching for us, trying to draw us into the warmth of His searchlight so we would place our identity and security in Him. He never gave up the challenge of clearing us out of our cozy corner of indifference. He kept looking, kept lighting lamps to illuminate our path. Once we caught His vision for our finances, we applied that same spirit of perseverance to paying off debt.

Being discovered by God for His purposes in the midst of our own story was humbling and terrifying. Light streaming in on our soul felt warm and safe while also raw and humiliating. We had made *so many* mistakes. Cue the stark spotlight on our financial idiocy. God still had a plan for our finances, and He never gave up on us.

While I related to the coin in the parable, I also felt a connection with the treasure-seeking widow. As I shared our story with more groups and we inched closer to our goal, I wanted to jump up and down, waving my arms and cheering, "Hey! I found something of outrageous value. I want to share it with you! I want to bless you because of what was found in our story. C'mon! You don't want to miss it!"

But let's not overlook the most important point of this parable. Jesus didn't come to earth to straighten out our finances. The most jaw-dropping sentence in this parable is this: "I tell you, there is rejoicing in the presence of the angels of God over one sinner who repents." If you remember nothing else in this book, if none of the financial or frugal tips stay with you, please don't miss this essential, eternal truth: God is the only source of true freedom in your life. Saving money, paying off debt, and balancing the books might all bring temporary satisfaction and might even clear the confusion in your life. But they will never eliminate the chaos in your soul.[3]

> God is the only source of true freedom in your life.

D-Free Day

Wednesday, March 28, 2012, was a good day; no, a very good day—though it didn't start differently from any other. A friend and I had jogged three and a half miles to Panera, where she treated me to lunch. When I got back home, it was time to tackle the stack of dirty dishes and the pile of laundry.

After folding clothes late that afternoon, I was sitting at the keyboard cranking out a blog post when Brian came home. After greeting me, he tossed a Meijer bag in my direction. Opening it, I found a package of undies. Don't think ooh-la-la; think basic Hanes six-pack. Let's just say the towels weren't the only thing in our house that were beginning to wear out. (Remember my excitement at the contents of that white trash bag?) I giggled anyway, knowing he had bought them because he knows I'm not good at spending money on myself, even in those days when I *needed* something.

I figured Brian was just encouraging me because I'd been battling doubt, anger, and fear over the past few weeks and we were still a month or so away from the finish line. But then he handed me a deposit slip. It showed that he had just deposited more than twice as much as we needed to pay off our final Sallie Mae installment. Turns out, a bonus had come in earlier than expected.

I stood up, fell into Brian's arms, and wept. It was hard to believe it was almost over. Four years of struggle—of scrimping every dime, of saying no dozens of times to others and ourselves, of endless number crunching, of feeling in bondage to debt that literally owned us. Everything was soon to change.

Like the woman who found the lost coin, we knew we wanted to share our news with our family and friends. So we quickly cleaned the area of our kitchen where we could shoot a video announcing the official slaying of our debt dragon. (We didn't care that the rest of the kitchen was a wreck.) After telling our girls the good news and asking a friend to come over to take the video and some photos, Brian and I sat at our kitchen table and logged into our Sallie Mae account. Our friend recorded Brian and me as we made our final payment.

We capped off the night by going out for dinner at Texas

Roadhouse, the restaurant our girls picked.[4] (Their choice was awesome because I had coupons good for two free kids' meals. Old habits die hard!)

The next day we posted the video on YouTube, calling it "A Royal Announcement," as a surprise for our friends, family, and blog readers. We had reached our goal about thirty days before we originally anticipated—three days before we hit the four-year anniversary of launching our battle against debt—and we were still in a state of shock.

A few weeks later, we traveled to Nashville, where we'd arranged to scream "We're debt-free!" live from Dave Ramsey's studios after he'd asked us a few questions on-air about our debt-slaying journey.[5] Once we were home, we immediately launched into debt-free party planning. We knew we wanted good music. We knew we wanted good food. We knew we wanted to celebrate with anyone who had encouraged us on our journey, whether we knew them or not. We knew we wanted to give away good gifts, things that had helped us so much—from the homemade cleaning products I mentioned in chapter 6 to books that had inspired us and more. We knew we wanted a record of who was there.

In mid-May, we hosted our party. Attendees drove from up to three hours away to be with us. We served fried chicken, and everyone brought a dish to share. In lieu of gifts, we had asked our party attendees to bring any loose change they could find in their cars and homes. Together we collected $100 to donate to Blood:Water Mission![6]

After Brian and I did some fun giveaways, a friend performed two songs written in our honor—"Sallie Mae Is Not My Lender," sung to the tune of "Billie Jean," and "The Grocery" (a tribute to my coupon binder) to the tune of Matthew West's "The Motions."[7]

My favorite remembrance from that day now hangs over the love seat in our living room. It's a four-foot-by-two-foot green canvas shaped like a dollar bill with the word *Freedom* scrawled across the top. In place of Washington's face are two crowns with our last name emblazoned beneath them. In the two top corners are the numbers 3 and 12, which represent the month and year we paid our final debt. At the bottom are words from one of our favorite Bible verses, Romans 13:8: "Owe nothing to anyone except love."

All over the canvas are words of congratulations and encouragement. Each brightly colored Sharpie greeting was penned by a reveler at our debt-free party. My favorite ones were written by children, some accompanied with little hearts and smiley faces. Reading all the scrawled messages was a great way to end the evening. Even today I relax and feel happy just thinking about our celebration because it brought such relief and fulfillment.

Even if you're not the partying type, I strongly encourage you to set an "endgame" goal for your own debt-slaying journey. On the days when you feel at your worst, you can cling to the vision of that experience, knowing that the end will come and it will be *epic*. Whether you decide on a vacation or a fancy meal or a phone call to someone special,

> I strongly encourage you to set an "endgame" goal for your own debt-slaying journey.

make plans to celebrate what God has done in your story. Be sure it will allow you to express your gratitude to those who have made a difference in your debt-slaying journey. To pause and reflect. To inspire others to take the same journey.

Life after Debt

In many ways, our lives have changed dramatically since paying off $127K in debt. In many ways, they have remained the same. In July 2012, Brian finally broke his restaurant-free streak. After fielding a bracket of sixty-four dining establishments (the majority of them local), we let blog readers vote on where he should eat first.

There were four divisions—fancy schmancy, Italimexinese, bovine, and Errbody Else, each with sixteen possible destinations. In the end, 3 Sisters Café won out. The lemon corncakes served with seasonal berries featured on the Food Network's *Diners, Drive-Ins, and Dives* did not disappoint. However, by the spring of the next year, Brian went on another six-month restaurant fast.

We purchased new pillows and towels. We returned to eating meat and even bumped up the grocery budget by fifteen dollars per week. We started buying toilet paper that's a little more expensive due to Brian's decree of "No more prison paper" after we became debt-free. I've returned to purchasing paper plates for our household. We went on a real vacation and a couple of short road trips. We purchased a car with cash.

Brian and I give each other gifts now, although they're still affordable and simple. We have an official budget for dining out and entertainment. I've even bought some new clothes, which has been nice but not nearly as exciting as I thought it would be. I discovered I actually love my old sweatshirts and yoga pants.

Most of our money-saving habits remained in place even after we paid off debt. We still use coupons. We still meal plan. We still pay with cash. We still garden. We still bargain. We still abide by the same principles we established to teach our children about money. We still have regular budget meetings. We still spend every Thursday night with our community group. We rarely turn on the TV. Instead of whacking away at the debt dragon, now we've built an emergency fund that could cover six months of living expenses for our family. We began pouring extra dollars into saving for retirement and building college funds for the Princesses.

It's so much more fun to watch savings climb rather than debt reduce. That money actually belongs to you and not someone else.

We've loved the ability to give away more of our income as well. We now choose to fully tithe. We also created an account we call the

"Generous Fund," which allows us to occasionally take people out to dinner, buy them books, or serve them in other practical ways. Not long ago, we were able to stock some college students' refrigerators, which was so fun! We gave away more money in the first year of being debt-free than we had ever given away in all the previous years of our marriage combined.

We've started making a concentrated effort toward paying off our mortgage—our new enemy. We owe much less on it than we've paid off already, so it doesn't seem like that far of a distant dream.

Time marches on and life is different. But the experience of paying off debt has marked us in a way that has forever changed our lives. Never again will we borrow. It's simply not an option. Credit cards and loans are a thing of the past. We left some of our "crazy" sacrifices behind. Others we know are essential for sustained financial success.

God has continued to broaden the platform from which we get to share our story. In December 2012, the *Wall Street Journal* e-mailed me about our debt-free party. Turns out, googling the term results in seeing my face. By the end of the month, we saw our story shared on a national level, which was so fun and a little bit bizarre. I still regularly blog, encouraging people to save money and slay debt. Also, I now appear weekly on the NBC affiliate in Indianapolis, sharing frugal life hacks and personal finance tips. I write a column for a local newspaper and through God's grace have had the opportunity to write this book to share our story. Plus, we've been blessed to speak with a number of amazing churches and groups, telling about our journey and spreading hope.

Writing Freedom in the Sand

Six months after we announced to the world that we were debt-free, I traced my finger on the ocean shore. In the sand I scratched out seven letters, F-R-E-E-D-O-M, and then I watched as each groove filled with foamy water. Glancing back, I saw my sweet little family and some of our dearest friends building sand castles near the beach house we had rented. I don't define many moments as perfect, but that sixty-second experience was one for the books.

I skipped around the letters written in the sand, knowing that God always had this plan in mind. To bring us out of bondage and into freedom. To surprise us with twists and turns in our story that we could never have dreamed, asked, or imagined. Salty air filled every square inch of my lungs. After days of struggle, frustration, and tears, I realized that each battle and every sacrifice had been worth it.

I had begun dreaming of standing in this very place four months before we made that last payment to Sallie Mae. I visualized myself standing on the other side of debt, taking a vacation paid for 100 percent with cash and not spent crashing at a friend's or family member's house. In my dreams, I could feel the sunshine on my face and hear the crash of the waves.

Now I was standing in that remote destination in North Carolina. I had trolled the Internet for the perfect beachfront house, one with four bedrooms and three baths to accommodate our friends and family. Each bedroom needed to face the ocean. A killer kitchen and a washer and dryer were high priorities. I wanted a home far from traffic and commerce, just a quiet place to gather our joy and watch the waves.

After some intense bargaining (we got a great deal!), narrowly avoiding car-sickness as we drove through West Virginia, and making a highly anticipated stop at a Southern chain known for its biscuits, we spent seven wonderful days inhaling sea air and exhaling words of praise. God had done so much for us.

Our family walked along the beach together holding hands, splashing in the waves. I was overwhelmed by God's expanse of grace for us all, far greater than the depths of the ocean. I couldn't help but think of Psalm 36:5-9, a passage that had always meant a lot to Brian and me:

Your unfailing love, O Lord, is as vast as the heavens;
 your faithfulness reaches beyond the clouds.
Your righteousness is like the mighty mountains,
 your justice like the ocean depths.
You care for people and animals alike, O Lord.
 How precious is your unfailing love, O God!
All humanity finds shelter
 in the shadow of your wings.
You feed them from the abundance of your own house,
 letting them drink from your river of delights.
For you are the fountain of life,
 the light by which we see. (NLT)

We were overwhelmed by the enormity of God's unfailing love and care. We had once been in the dark; now He was the light by which we saw.

All that week we paused. We played. We prayed. We savored a moment given to us with some of the people we loved most. Also, I got to eat fresh seafood. For me, our time on the North Carolina shore was a glimpse of heaven on earth.

In the evenings, we left the sliding door open and listened to the waves crash while we did many of the same things that had sustained our souls during those years of paying off debt. We read books. We put together puzzles. We watched silly movies. We played games.

From the moment we shared our story for the very first time, God began rippling it forward in ways that have often left us speechless. From the local newscast to the *Wall Street Journal*, He began broadcasting what He had done for us and through us.

Even now, when He sends another opportunity to share, we stand in awe, as if we are watching the waves of the ocean. We're filled with a deep sense of the enormity of His lovingkindness, and gratitude floods our souls. How could it be that such messed-up people get to bear His image and share His story?

Oh, Money-Saving Lords and Ladies, how I wish I could place freedom from debt in a bottle for you, sparkling with beauty just like the sea glass from that very beach that now sits on my bookshelf. But if I could offer you that gift, you would miss the twists and turns, the grace-filled surprises, and the eternal lessons of contentment. After all, our God "is able to do immeasurably more than all we ask or imagine, according to his power that is at work within us" (Ephesians 3:20, NIV).

You don't want our debt-slaying journey. It would be a cheap imitation of your own.

Endings Are Better than Beginnings

At her urging, I tell my friend Kayla about the events that led up to our unforgettable vacation. She sits across from me at the coffee shop and delicately sips her hot cocoa, which is still a little too steamy. "I love hearing others' stories of becoming debt-free. I get so emotional just listening," she says. "But you see, it's just so hard to begin. We don't really have that much debt. You guys could probably pay it off in a weekend. I don't know why we can't kick-start our own journey."

I know that my friend is exactly right. Screaming that you're debt-free is much more fun than starting after the debt dragon on day one. Debt-free parties, vacations, and celebrations fill us with excitement and joy, even when they aren't our own. The beginning of a debt-slaying journey, while exciting in many ways, occurs with much less fanfare than the ending. No one offers words of "Atta girl! Atta boy!" "You did it!" "Congratulations!" No one sings songs or signs canvases. No one drives hundreds of miles to see you and share in your joy. Commencing your journey of commitment is certainly one instance in life when these sage words from Ecclesiastes ring true:

"The end of a matter is better than its beginning, and patience is better than pride" (Ecclesiastes 7:8, NIV).

Beginnings require you to move in a new direction, to reorient your life. Beginnings seek to break old habits and put new patterns in their place. Beginnings are painful. For there to be new life and freedom, something else must die. Beginnings bring grief.

I can't tell you how many times I have avoided beginning because I know it will hurt. From difficult decisions about jobs to complex conversations about relationships, beginning stinks worse than that sippy cup filled with milk from three weeks ago that you found under the car seat in the middle of July. Beginnings are that bad.

This is old news to you now (assuming you actually read chapter 6), but when the King of Free and I were first married, we weren't the best at keeping our apartment in tip-top shape. In fact, we once pulled out the bed of our couch in the living room and slept on it instead of clearing off the bed in our bedroom. What's that you say? Was our bedroom flooded so we weren't able to sleep there? Did our ceiling cave in and create an enormous mess? No. Our bed and bedroom were simply trashed. It looked like the Rolling Stones had partied there all night. I cannot for the life of me remember what we had been doing, but let me assure you we have always been incredibly boring people. There was no reason for our room to have been such a pit.

Seriously, how lazy do you have to be to avoid just shoving all the dirty laundry and junk onto the floor? It probably took more energy for us to make up the couch in the living room than it would have taken for us to simply clean up our own mess. And let me be frank: the pull-out couch was not comfortable. More than one spring poked up through the three-inch mattress. We knew that. We were avoiding cleaning our room like eight-year-old kids, and it literally ended up physically hurting us both. It was a ridiculous, painful situation of our own making.

Can you see the metaphor I'm drawing here? Even though it's difficult to begin a debt-slaying journey and you'd probably rather daydream about the endgame, you don't want to endure another night sleeping on the pull-out couch.

It's okay to be afraid. It's okay to feel as if this season is never going to end. It's okay to feel overwhelmed, frustrated, and confused. Those are your feelings, and you have them for a reason. It's *not* okay, though, to wallow in those feelings, doing nothing. In the end, work—hard work—is what pays off debt. Remember, when you are afraid, God is very near, ready to take your hand and do the unthinkable and impossible. Trust Him to battle your feelings of insecurity as you take your first steps toward freedom.

Final Words and a Battle Cry

We're all tempted to think that our lives are inconsequential. That we're daily tasked with doing the mundane while more qualified individuals get to have all the fun. Granted, we might not ever get to scale Mount Everest. (Come to think of it, I saw a documentary on that once and it did *not* look like fun, so count me out.) And we might never hear a stadium of people chanting our names.

Those lies and whispers often intensify.

You can't do anything right.
It will never be enough.
Everyone can do that.

Such taunts are simply not true. With grace, you have the potential for greatness. You can allow your story to ripple and change the lives of others.

Back to that oversized canvas painted like a dollar bill hanging in our living room. It is an overwhelming symbol of the ripples we make in one another's lives. Three of the families who signed the canvas are now debt-free themselves. Another is close to paying off their final credit card. One of them invited us to their mortgage-burning party.

Everyone has a story. Everyone's story ripples. Whose waves are you feeling, and which ones are you sending forth? Proverbs 13:20 says, "Whoever walks with the wise becomes wise, but the companion of fools will suffer harm" (ESV). Please note, this is not saying you will become a fool if you keep company with fools. You will suffer harm. But if you walk with wise people, not only will you avoid such harm, but you will also become wise, just like them.

Dragons can be beaten. You have more strength (God's power) than you realize, less debt than you think, and everything it takes to kick that debt dragon in the teeth and to eventually boot it out the door. You're fighting not just for bottom lines and account balances, but for your marriage, your children, your friends, your family, and your very soul.

May you realize that you are not alone in this battle.
May you recognize that dragons can be beaten.
May you step into your own story.
May you find true forgiveness for your debts.
May you name your debt and turn from it, running
    toward God.
May you gain freedom and joy through your budget.
May you discover "oil" overflowing in small jars as you realize
    that God has blessed you with enough.
May you delight in the sweetness of frugality.
May you be filled with perseverance in the moments when you
    need it most.
May your marriage sing with financial harmony.
May you crowd out the naysayers and draw nearer to like-
    minded debt slayers.

May you be surprised by God's goodness and reminded that He
is for you in this journey.

May you focus on delighting in the blessing of your children.

May you teach your children to be wise with money, learning
from your mistakes.

May you work long hours in pursuit of a greater goal, knowing
the task is only for a season.

May you share your story with others who feel alone in their
battle so that they can gain victory too.

May you slay the debt dragon.

It's time to gear up, Money-Saving Lords and Ladies. To act like
grown-ups and dig into that mess. Avoiding the situation will only
make it worse. The pain will be greater with each passing day. The
beginning will be more difficult. *Remember, there is no good time to
begin paying off debt. There is only today.*

Let me leave you with a special blessing, one that God com-
manded the priests to proclaim over the people of Israel as they made
final preparations to enter the Promised Land—and to take on their
enemies. God had promised them a new beginning, to move out
of the darkness of oppression and into the light of freedom. Sound
familiar?

The LORD bless you and keep you;

the LORD make his face to shine upon you and be gracious to
you;

the LORD lift up his countenance upon you and give you peace.

NUMBERS 6:24-26, ESV

Acknowledgments

BEAR WITH ME—this list will be longer than you probably want to wade through. What can I say? I'm an overthanker.

Dearest Brian, you steal my heart each and every day, JCPenney boy. What an amazing adventure being married to you has been and continues to be. Even after fifteen years, I'm still kind of surprised at how much you love me even though you truly know me. If it weren't for your vision for our family and finances, there would be no book. Thanks for putting your hand on the small of my back. I love you.

Anna and Zoe, life must not be easy when your mom wears a plastic crown and does countless other wacky things. You are my favorite works of art. My heart longs for you to follow Jesus in your own unique ways your whole life long, bringing grace and redemption into the world through everything you do. Thank you for being the best Anna and Zoe you can be. I love you.

Mom and Dad, God only knows where I'd be without you. You've sent me on more grace-drenched adventures over the last thirty-seven years than I can count. My favorite one so far is the one that launched this book. Your careful, wise direction, your kind hearts, and your undaunted belief in me knock me over and turn me inside out. Thank you for your godly examples of marriage, faith, and living life for all it's worth. I love you.

Ron and Sally, you raised the boy who became my man. You love me like your own child. You continually shower down love on my daughters, soft and gentle. I could never thank you enough. I love you.

Big hugs and high fives to our extended family: brothers, their wives, nieces, nephews, cousins, aunts, uncles, grandparents. Your encouragement, belief in us, and words of wisdom mean more than you'll ever know. Thank you. We love you.

To our community group, you have surrounded us with unfaltering encouragement, prayer, wisdom, loyalty, uncontrollable laughter, love for our children, and passionate vision for God's plan for our lives together. May we eat cupcakes and make investments forever. Can we "beginue" to love God, love people, and show up? The best is yet to come. We love you.

One rainy August morning, Margaret Feinberg and I walked along the sea. I still kind of can't believe it wasn't a dream. She passionately spoke these words into my life: "You're going to write a book, and you're going to do it now." Part of me was encouraged; part of me thought, *Yeah, right.* Thank you, sweet friend, for seeing something my eyes couldn't glimpse and encouraging me in ways no one else could, in the midst of your own battles. My heart will forever be grateful.

Special thanks to the Re:Write Conference, everyone at The Fedd Agency, and the amazing people at Tyndale Momentum. Your belief in this work, your encouragement, and your grace for a rookie author are astounding. Thank you for this amazing opportunity to share our story and spread hope. I especially appreciate the enthusiasm and understanding of Esther Fedorkevich and Lisa Schmidt, who answered an unlimited number of what were probably ridiculous and neurotic first-time author questions.

Big grammatically correct hugs and kisses to my phenomenal editor, Kim Miller. There's no one else I'd rather put together a jigsaw puzzle with. Your encouragement, guidance, and vision helped bring stories out of my soul that I had forgotten to remember, let alone tell. Thank you for your encouragement and help in refining our story.

High fives with lots of exclamation marks to Jillian VandeWege, whose excitement and wisdom helped me expand on ideas of how to get this book into your hands. Appreciative squeezes for the lovely Sharon Leavitt, who helped me comb through every detail and quickly answered each of my questions, no matter how small, from the very first day. Special thanks to Jan Long Harris and Sarah Atkinson for their watchful eyes, decades of publishing know-how, and undergirding belief that our story needed to be told. I'm so grateful for the mad design skills of Nicole Grimes, who used visuals to sprinkle hope on every page. I greatly appreciate the intentional work of Annette Hayward, the copy editor who made sure I didn't say anything I didn't mean. Let's just say she cleared up more than one "oops" on my part and didn't laugh too hard in the process. Last but certainly not least, Nancy Clausen, Yolanda Sidney, and Andrea Martin, thank you for lending your guidance, expertise, and excitement in the realms of marketing and publicity.

To the many communities who make me who I am, fill my life with joy and laughter, and stretch me beyond my comfort zone, I am overwhelmed with deep gratitude. Thank you to the Pastor A-Team—Scot, Brodie, Ryan, Devin, and Michael—five guys who have freely given their time and wisdom to shape this work and pray for its impact. Thanks to the Stones Crossing Church community for over a decade of practical love, encouragement, wisdom, learning, laughter, and joy. Thank you to the Indy Geek Girls who "get" my addiction to social media, collectively know more about blogging than Google, and daily make me smile with their lens on the world. Thank you to my sisters in Christ who read the same books, love the same authors, and frequent the same blogs. Your whispers of "me too" make me feel less crazy or at least thankful that you are crazy with me.

Royal thanks to the Money-Saving Lords and Ladies in the Court of the Queen of Free who have traveled this road with me from the beginning, through its highs and lows, its victories and defeats. May you be bright lights in the lives of others who are casting off the chains of debt.

Slaying the Debt Dragon Playlist

I HAVE ALWAYS LOVED MUSIC. I strongly believe that the power of words and a melody can fuel a journey. Songs of freedom powered both our debt-slaying journey and the writing of this book. Here are a few of the songs that we drew upon to give us strength.

- Tenth Avenue North, "The Struggle," *The Struggle*
- Mandisa, "Overcomer," *Overcomer*
- Building 429, "Where I Belong," *Listen to the Sound*
- Chris Tomlin, "Amazing Grace (My Chains Are Gone)," *See the Morning*
- The Script, "Hall of Fame [Clean]," *#3*
- All Sons and Daughters, "I Am Set Free," *Brokenness Aside EP No. 1*
- Desperation Band, "I Am Free," *From the Rooftops*
- Matt Redman, "We Are the Free," *10,000 Reasons*
- Hillsong United, "Freedom Is Here," *Across the Earth: Tear Down the Walls*
- Rend Collective Experiment, "Build Your Kingdom Here," *Campfire*
- Mary Mary, "Shackles (Praise You)," *Go Get It*

- Charlie Hall, "Mystery," *The Bright Sadness*
- Phil Wickham, "This Is the Day," *Response*
- Britt Nicole, "Ready or Not," *Gold*
- Travis Tritt, "It's a Great Day to Be Alive," *Down the Road I Go*
- Gungor, "Beautiful Things," *Beautiful Things*
- Francesca Battistelli, "Free to Be Me," *My Paper Heart*
- Vertical Church Band, "I'm Going Free (Jailbreak)," *The Rock Won't Move*

Slaying the Debt Dragon Reading List

SOME OF MY best friends in life have been books. While paying off debt, Brian and I read anything and everything we could get our hands on that we thought would be encouraging and helpful. We've continued to read in the years following. This reading list provides a few possible literary companions for your debt-slaying journey.

Money

Felber, Terry. *The Legend of the Monk and the Merchant: Principles for Successful Living.* Nashville: Word Publishing, 2004.

Ramsey, Dave. *The Total Money Makeover.* Nashville: Thomas Nelson, 2007.

Scurlock, James D. *Maxed Out: Hard Times, Easy Credit, and the Era of Predatory Lenders.* New York: Scribner, 2007.

Stanley, Thomas J., and William D. Danko. *The Millionaire Next Door: The Surprising Secrets of America's Wealthy.* Atlanta: Longstreet, 1996.

Stanley, Thomas J. *Stop Acting Rich . . . and Start Living Like a Real Millionaire.* Hoboken, NJ: Wiley, 2009.

Marriage and Parenting

Barna, George. *Revolutionary Parenting.* Carol Stream, IL: Tyndale Momentum, 2010.

Dungy, Tony and Lauren Dungy. *Uncommon Marriage: Learning about Lasting Love and Overcoming Life's Obstacles Together.* Carol Stream, IL: Tyndale Momentum, 2014.

Joiner, Reggie, and Carey Nieuwhof. *Parenting beyond Your Capacity: Connect Your Family to a Wider Community.* Colorado Springs, CO: David C. Cook, 2010.

Keller, Timothy J., and Kathy Keller. *The Meaning of Marriage: Facing the Complexities of Commitment with the Wisdom of God*. New York: Dutton, 2011.

Meeker, Margaret J. *Strong Fathers, Strong Daughters: 10 Secrets Every Father Should Know*. Washington, DC: Regnery, 2006.

Ramsey, Dave, and Rachel Cruze. *Smart Money Smart Kids: Raising the Next Generation to Win with Money*. Brentwood, TN: Lampo, 2014.

Sun Tzu. *The Art of War*. Translated with an introduction by Samuel B. Griffith. London: Oxford University Press, 1971.

Faith

DeMuth, Mary E. *The Wall around Your Heart: How Jesus Heals You When Others Hurt You*. Nashville: Thomas Nelson, 2013.

Feinberg, Margaret. *Scouting the Divine: My Search for God in Wine, Wool, and Wild Honey*. Grand Rapids, MI: Zondervan, 2009.

Feinberg, Margaret. *Wonderstruck: Awaken to the Nearness of God*. Brentwood, TN: Worthy, 2012.

Freeman, Emily P. *A Million Little Ways: Uncover the Art You Were Made to Live*. Grand Rapids, MI: Revell, 2013.

Gerth, Holley. *You're Made for a God-Sized Dream: Opening the Door to All God Has for You*. Grand Rapids, MI: Revell, 2013.

Goff, Bob. *Love Does: Discover a Secretly Incredible Life in an Ordinary World*. Nashville: Thomas Nelson, 2012.

Groeschel, Craig. *Weird: Because Normal Isn't Working*. Grand Rapids, MI: Zondervan, 2011.

Keller, Timothy J. *Encounters with Jesus: Unexpected Answers to Life's Biggest Questions*. New York: Penguin Group, 2013.

Stanley, Andy. *The Principle of the Path: How to Get from Where You Are to Where You Want to Be*. Nashville: Thomas Nelson, 2008.

Wright, N. T. *Following Jesus: Biblical Reflections on Discipleship*. Grand Rapids, MI: Eerdmans, 1995.

Generosity and Contentment

Blanchard, Kenneth H., and S. Truett Cathy. *The Generosity Factor: Discover the Joy of Giving Your Time, Talent, and Treasure*. Grand Rapids, MI: Zondervan, 2002.

Hatmaker, Jen. *7: An Experimental Mutiny against Excess*. Nashville: B&H Publishing Group, 2012.

Keller, Timothy J. *Generous Justice: How God's Grace Makes Us Just*. New York: Dutton, Penguin Group (USA), 2010.

Sanders, Tim. *Today We Are Rich: Harnessing the Power of Total Confidence*. Carol Stream, IL: Tyndale, 2011.

Stanley, Andy. *How to Be Rich: It's Not What You Have, It's What You Do with What You Have*. Grand Rapids, MI: Zondervan, 2013.

Leadership

Acuff, Jonathan M. *Start: Punch Fear in the Face, Escape Average, Do Work That Matters.* Brentwood, TN: Lampo, 2013.

Collins, James C. *Good to Great: Why Some Companies Make the Leap . . . and Others Don't.* New York: HarperBusiness, 2001.

Gladwell, Malcolm. *Outliers: The Story of Success.* New York: Little, Brown, 2008.

Godin, Seth. *Tribes: We Need You to Lead Us.* New York: Portfolio, 2008.

Ramsey, Dave. *EntreLeadership: 20 Years of Practical Business Wisdom from the Trenches.* New York: Howard, 2011.

Sinek, Simon. *Start with Why: How Great Leaders Inspire Everyone to Take Action.* New York: Portfolio, 2009.

Discussion Guide

Chapter 1: Once upon a Time

1. Consider your own "once upon a time." Where did your journey with money and debt begin?

2. What choices did you make in your financial past that you had no idea would affect your present condition?

3. "There is no good time to begin paying off debt. There is only today." How does this statement speak to you? Have you been waiting for an ideal moment to launch your debt-slaying quest?

4. How are debt and forgiveness uniquely tied together in your story?

5. What sorts of dreams do you have for your money once you are debt-free? What will you do? Where will you go? How might you make the world a better place?

Chapter 2: Debt-Defying Duos

1. Leading and being led is a delicate dance. Where have you seen this play out well before? Where have you seen couples struggle with this principle?

2. Casting a vision for your spouse to buy into the process of paying off debt can be challenging. Which item of the "what not to do" list is the biggest challenge for you? Which behavior do you find yourself returning to without realizing it?

3. "The death of communication is the birth of resentment." When has this been true in your marriage or other relationships?

4. What negative associations have you had with the word *frugal* in the past? What ridiculous ways have you heard of others living in a manner they considered frugal?

5. How does knowing that the word *frugal* has a very sweet origin change your perspective?

6. When have you felt scarcity—the fear that you would be left alone and without something you longed for—in your life? What have you done to cope with it?

Chapter 3: Starting-Line Strategies

1. Have you ever run a race? How might paying off debt be like running a race?

2. "Society wants to make you think that debt is neutral—even natural." In what ways have you accepted cultural norms or understandings of debt? Can you relate to Luke's, Nickole's, or Stacey's story?

3. Names have power. Has anyone ever called you by the wrong name? How did it make you feel?

4. Go back and read the sentences about Fred Johnson on page 36. How does personifying debt with the name "Fred Johnson" change your view of debt?

5. How has fear held you back in your debt-slaying journey? Have you ever thought about the idea that God is nearby in the midst of fear?

6. Look at the Scripture passages on pages 43–44. As you consider beginning your debt journey, which one leaps off the page at you, speaking most powerfully to the anxiety or fears you face today?

7. When have you made a change that was too drastic or unsustainable? What was the result?

Chapter 4: Budgets Are Your Battle-Ax

1. How has your view of budgeting negatively impacted your practice of budgeting? Have you seen budgeting as fingers around your neck or as wings to help you fly? Talk about ways you could change your perspective.

2. Which tools are you most comfortable using to budget? Traditional paper and pencil? Technology?

3. Have you found a certain budgeting method to be not successful for you? Why is it not wise to return to this same method again, expecting a different result?

4. Which of the strategies to improve weekly budget meetings do you already practice? Which has the most potential to help you grow and stretch? What strategy would you add?

5. What budget category would be the easiest for you to convert to a cash envelope system? Which would be most difficult?

6. "Your enemy is debt, not the budget." How would your current financial journey change if you began to view your budget as your friend rather than the bad guy?

7. What are you doing to safeguard the many valuables God has blessed you with so that they don't end up in a yard sale?

Chapter 5: At the Royal Table

1. Have you ever "meal planned" before?

   a. If you currently plan your meals, what's your typical strategy or approach? What tools do you use?

   b. If you've never planned your meals, which of the specific methods do you think would work best for you? Paper and pencil? App? Online service?

2. How would your dining-out experience change if it became a scheduled part of your meal plan?

3. Which of the Grocery Store Ten Commandments could you relate to the most? What other mandates would you add for your own personal top ten?

4. Do you use coupons? How might you change your current practice to make it more effective, given some of the tips shared?

5. How much money do you think you could save if you packed lunches for everyone in your family? What would you do with the money you saved?

6. In what areas of your life have you been making "wellllllllll" statements, underplaying the good gifts you already have?

Chapter 6: Keeping the Castle Clean

1. Do you enjoy cleaning? Why or why not?

2. Have you ever thought about the idea of running your

household as a business? How would you change your household systems if you were being paid? Would you be "fired" from your job?

3. Have you viewed utility bills as static or negotiable? Which of the tips in this section surprised you?

4. In what ways have you learned to save money when it comes to doing laundry? How might you improve?

5. Do you make your own household cleaners?

a. If you do, share a recipe with others in your group.

b. Which recipes from this chapter would you like to attempt to make?

6. How could you be generous even while paying off debt?

Chapter 7: Formidable Foes and Fellow Debt Slayers

1. What's the funniest misunderstanding with a preschooler you've ever had (or heard about)?

2. Has anyone been confused by your pursuit to pay off debt? What sorts of questions have they asked or what expressions of concern have they issued?

3. Have you struggled with wanting to be like "everyone else"? What safeguards can you place in your life to keep you from the temptation of comparison?

4. How are your friends influencing your life for better or worse?

5. Do you currently have a group of like-minded debt slayers encouraging you in your journey? If not, where might you find such a group?

6. How can being a cheerleader for someone else bring joy and strength to your own journey? Who are you currently encouraging to reach their financial goals?

7. What money "genes" have you inherited from your parents? How does knowing your children might inherit your money practices change your perspective?

Chapter 8: Of Princes and Princesses

1. What was the very first thing you did when you discovered you were going to be a parent? What fears did you have?

2. Have you or your child ever imagined there was a monster under the bed? How did you respond? How might even the smallest financial worries between you and your spouse fester into a bigger problem for your child? In what ways could you intentionally combat the money "monster under the bed" syndrome in your household?

3. Can you relate to the pity party Cherie threw herself when her family began paying off debt, fearing that her children were going to "pay" for her mistakes? Why is that guilt so difficult to overcome?

4. Where have you discovered unexpected blessings with your family or provisions for your family's needs?

5. What's the craziest kids' birthday party you've ever attended? Which birthday party budgeting strategy would you like to use with your children? What other ways do you save on birthdays?

6. Do you love to give gifts? In what ways could you exercise creativity while paying off debt to still give gifts without spending a great deal of money?

7. How do your children earn money in your household? Do you have an intentional plan to help them learn the vital lessons of giving, saving, and spending? Which of Cherie's strategies would you like to try?

8. It's been said that in the journey of parenting, the days are long but the years are short. How does a long-term perspective of your children as future grown-ups influence the ways you attempt to impact their lives?

Chapter 9: Joy for the Journey: A Benediction

1. When has God shown up in an unexpected place to remind you how much He cares about even the smallest details of your life?

2. Celebrating what was once lost but is now found is a recurring metaphor in Jesus' teachings. Coins, sheep, and sons all stand as reminders of His great love for us. What have you "found" as a result of paying off debt and reorganizing your finances?

3. In what ways will you celebrate financial freedom?

4. "The end of a matter is better than its beginning, and patience is better than pride" (Ecclesiastes 7:8, NIV). How have you found this verse to be true in your own life? What sorts of struggles prevent us from beginning a challenging journey?

5. Why is it important to contemplate how the ripples of our lives touch the lives of others?

6. How can we suffer if we become the companion of fools?

7. "There is no good time to begin paying off debt. There is only today." What will you do today to begin (or continue) your debt-slaying journey?

8. What do you consider to be the most important change in your daily financial practices after reading this book?

Notes

Introduction

1. Author Neil Gaiman paraphrased G. K. Chesterton's longer quotation found in *Tremendous Trifles*, which was first published in 1909. In chapter 17, "The Red Angel," Chesterton says: "Fairy tales, then, are not responsible for producing in children fear, or any of the shapes of fear; fairy tales do not give the child the idea of the evil or the ugly; that is in the child already, because it is in the world already. Fairy tales do not give the child his first idea of bogey. What fairy tales give the child is his first clear idea of the possible defeat of bogey. The baby has known the dragon intimately ever since he had an imagination. What the fairy tale provides for him is a St. George to kill the dragon. Exactly what the fairy tale does is this: it accustoms him for a series of clear pictures to the idea that these limitless terrors had a limit, that these shapeless enemies have enemies in the knights of God, that there is something in the universe more mystical than darkness, and stronger than strong fear."

Chapter 1: Once upon a Time

1. To read more about the challenges in families where both parents work, see Elizabeth Warren and Amelia Warren Tyagi, *The Two-Income Trap: Why Middle-Class Mothers and Fathers Are Going Broke* (New York: Basic Books, 2003).

2. For the record, we've purchased numerous copies of *The Total Money Makeover* since then, and it's our go-to gift for any graduation or wedding. I'm hoping that grants us absolution. Side note: if you're at all familiar with Dave Ramsey and have any amount of debt, he's the type of guy you want to both bear-hug *and* stare down with the stink eye. It's funny how we can both embrace and push back on our own darkness when it's dragged into the light.

3. I'm often asked a number of questions about how we paid off so much debt so quickly. Did we cash out our retirement? Did we inherit or win a large sum of

money? Did we consolidate our debt? Did we sell a major item like a vehicle? The answer to all of the above is no. We nickeled-and-dimed our way into six figures of debt with really nothing to show for it and then nickeled-and-dimed our way back out again.

4. Oh, my friends who like their grammar squeaky clean, I need to apologize. I realize that technically the correct terms are "Princess Elder" and "Princess Younger" since there is no third princess in the mix. However, every time I heard "Princess Elder" it conjured up images of an ancient wizard or a high-ranking officer in a secret society. So with an apologetic curtsy, I acknowledge and honor your grammar purism while breaking the rules and sticking with the royal titles I've always used on my blog.

5. Esther 4:14, NIV

Chapter 2: Debt-Defying Duos

1. When attending a conference in 1999, my husband, Brian, jotted down the words of one of the speakers, Mike Silva, who said, "The death of dialogue is the birth of resentment."

2. The full quotation is "There are two ways to get enough. One is to continue to accumulate more and more. The other is to desire less." G. K. is my homeboy.

Chapter 3: Starting-Line Strategies

1. No Fred Johnsons were harmed in the writing of this chapter.

2. My apologies to the Fred Johnsons of the world. I am quite positive that each of you is a delightful and amazing person. I promise I'm only using your name as an illustrative example and have no intentions of besmirching your outstanding character. My next book just might be *Why You Should Be More Like Fred Johnson*, but for now, please accept my humble apologies.

3. Jeffrey Dew, Sonya Britt, and Sandra Huston, "Examining the Relationship between Financial Issues and Divorce," *Family Relations* 61, no. 4 (October 2012): 615–628.

4. Joshua 1:9, NIV. After spending many years in children's ministry, Brian and I can't recite this verse without singing it.

5. Emphasis added. The Bible tells us not to fear more than 365 times! Three other such passages that I particularly appreciate are Matthew 14:26-27; Luke 1:12-14; and Revelation 1:16-18.

6. To learn about all seven steps in great detail, check out "The Seven Baby Steps" at www.daveramsey.com/new/baby-steps (accessed April 24, 2014).

7. John Trent, *The 2 Degree Difference: How Little Things Can Change Everything* (Nashville: B&H Publishing, 2006).

Chapter 4: Budgets Are Your Battle-Ax

1. I also once shared this tip in a newspaper article. Said newspaper article was read by my pastor's sixth-grade son, who exclaimed, "Why would Mrs. Lowe say

that?!" Note to self: if you ever want sixth-grade boys to look you in the eye again, don't share this story with them. My apologies to the sixth-grade boys who read this book and are now reading this endnote.

2. Computers have long been a part of my life. As a kid, one of my biggest joys was to type in the monthly BASIC programming from my *3-2-1 Contact* magazine to create a smiley face or a simple computer game on the screen. I'm a geek and I know it. So it's not a surprise that this method of budgeting comes most naturally to me.

3. Christians believe in giving a percentage of income (generally 10 percent) every month to their local church. It's not a tax or a payment to God in hopes of gaining His good favor. I've known those who don't attend church to misunderstand this practice as "dues" given to a religious organization. Instead, tithing is a way to sacrifice part of your income, acknowledging that all blessings, monetary and otherwise, come from God, the giver of all good things. Through giving, we joyfully show our gratitude and enable the church to make a difference in the world, drawing more people toward the compelling love of Jesus. Tithing can be controversial (How much? Gross vs. net? Is it a sin not to tithe?).

I'm no biblical scholar, but my heart breaks when I talk to families who long to give but cannot do that and pay their bills. I'm not talking about the cable bill or the cell phone bill, but the grocery bill. I love the wisdom of Timothy Keller, who teaches that tithing should be our aim, but that we should give until we feel a sacrifice. (By the way, Keller also points out that for some people, 10 percent is too small a sacrifice.)

Can I be boldly honest with you? In the heat of our battle against debt, Brian and I felt the sacrifice of giving sooner than we do now. Though we didn't give a set percentage to our church every week as we were paying off debt, we found ways to give by serving others with our talents. There was sacrifice involved and we certainly felt it, even if it wasn't a full "tithe" in the eyes of most. Maybe we were out of line. Maybe you feel differently. I'm not saying we made the best choice, nor am I dictating that this is the path for you to walk. This is just my honest explanation of how we handled this soul-searching decision.

One of the beautiful parts of becoming debt-free is the enhanced ability we now have to give to others, including the traditional method of tithing and even giving beyond that percentage.

For some of the wisest, most encouraging words on tithing, I encourage you visit the following site to read, study, and listen with an open heart: http:/www .redeemer.com/learn/resources_by_topic/generosity/stewardship/.

Timothy Keller has specific words about paying off debt and tithing in the last video, entitled "Wealth," here: www.redeemer.com/learn/resources_by_topic /generosity/generosity_sermon_series/generosity_questions_and_answers.This sermon series also explains generosity well: www.redeemer.com/learn/resources _by_topic/generosity/generosity_sermon_series.

4. Once we were debt-free, we created an emergency car fund for car repairs and the purchase of a new car.

5. While many personal finance experts recommend this strategy for monthly home budgets, I first learned about it from Dave Ramsey's teachings.

6. Gregory Karp, "Cash vs. Credit Mindset," *Chicago Tribune*, December 15, 2011, http://articles.chicagotribune.com/2011-12-15/news/sc-cons-1215-karpspend-20111210_1_credit-cards-card-balances-debit-cards (accessed April 24, 2014).

7. I carry the black-and-white wallet and *love* it. See www.thriftyzippers.com.

Chapter 5: At the Royal Table

1. 2 Kings 4:2, italics added

2. Retail employees, please don't hate me. This is not a regular practice of mine, nor am I suggesting it for others. It was a one-time event, and I felt *horrible* about it (still do). I am usually very intentional about putting items back or handing them to the cashier upon checkout with an apologetic "We don't need this after all; I am so sorry." I have horrible guilt if I place an item in the wrong place—I dwell on it for days. I also have issues with not placing my cart back in the corral. But that's another story for another day.

3. Not that I've ever snapped a little girl's head off and placed ice cream and three bags of potato chips in my cart willy-nilly because for the love of all, can we just get out of here and go home and *eat* already! I'd rather you picture me softly humming a hymn as I gently push my cart through the aisles wearing my best dress and heels, waving to my neighbors and instructing my children on the joy and beauty that is life.

4. I still know my best friend from sixth grade's phone number and birthday: 397-2394 and September 20. No peeking on Facebook necessary.

5. Thomas J. Stanley, PhD, *The Millionaire Mind* (Kansas City, MO: Andrews McMeel Publishing, 2001), 277–278.

6. Lest you think my husband is a complete killjoy or enforced his extreme frugality upon the rest of our family, I want you to know that he did not require the rest of us to abstain from restaurants while he did. It was his choice. He sat through business lunches without eating. We went on short road trips where he did not eat at restaurants. He was an absolute oak in his personal choice. On occasion, when we had budgeted for it, our family still dined out. He simply sat and chatted with us rather than partaking of the food. It turned out to be a *huge* blessing because he would attend to the needs of our children while I actually got to eat. Parents know that you have to either gobble down your food first and then attend to children or eat cold food after the other parent has rapidly consumed his or hers. And of course right after your food arrives, someone *always* has to go to the bathroom. It's not very much fun. Now that Brian eats at restaurants, I kinda wish he'd quit again.

7. You don't have to give up meat to pay off debt. This was something we felt called to do to speed our process. We began by eating meat only on weekends. We then

progressed to not purchasing it at all. Princess Eldest protested. She really likes cheeseburgers.

Chapter 6: Keeping the Castle Clean

1. Washing soda is found in the laundry detergent aisle, typically with the powdered detergents. Borax and washing soda are nothing new. Your grandma or great-grandma probably used them regularly.

2. You can grate the soap with your good ole cheese grater. It's fine to use the grater on foods again after you wash it or put it in the dishwasher. I have heard of others using Fels-Naptha soap too. It's another "classic cleaner" that has been around for decades. To chop it into small pieces, you might need a food processor because it's much harder and more dense than Ivory.

3. Thanks to Grandma Thelma, I love Erma Bombeck. Every time I spent time at my grandparents' home, I pored over paperbacks by Bombeck for hours in the guest bedroom. Recently I stumbled onto the idea that her style of humor on everyday life was the forerunner to mom blogging. I was completely absorbed in her mom humor long before I ever dreamt of having a child. Here's to you, Erma, for keeping it real before it was cool to keep it real, and here's to you, Grandma Thelma, for letting a ten-year-old kid read real books.

4. I know you think I'm seriously bonkers here, but you can use toothpaste to clean your jewelry—gold, white gold, sterling, or tarnished silver. Avoid the whitening, anti-tartar, and gel varieties and opt for plain old cheap (no added silica) toothpaste. Use an old toothbrush to scrub the piece, rinse it with water, and then dry it with a soft cloth. Or you can use another favorite recipe of mine—1 cup of hot water (microwaved or heated on the stove), 1 tablespoon of salt, 1 tablespoon of baking soda, and 1 tablespoon of dishwashing liquid, like Dawn. Line a cereal bowl with a piece of aluminum foil. Pour hot water in the bowl. Add the other ingredients. They will bubble up. (Science is cool!) Then place your jewelry on top of the foil. Let it sit for five to ten minutes. Rinse with cool water, scrub with an old toothbrush if necessary, and dry with a soft cloth. It really works! Your royal jewels will be super sparkly. Discard the solution, which doubles as a great drain cleaner. As a side note, from everything I've read, the second recipe is *not* advised for silver and soft stones like pearls or opals.

5. I found our current dishwashing detergent recipe on Pinterest in several places, so I'm not sure who deserves to be credited. Mix one 76-ounce box of borax, one 55-ounce box of washing soda, 3 cups of Epsom salts (found in the pharmacy), and 24 small packets of lemonade drink mix (think unsweetened Kool-Aid). The number one ingredient in the drink mix is citric acid, which will do the heavy lifting when it comes to getting your dishes spic and span. Be sure to keep the detergent in an airtight container and avoid getting it wet because it has a tendency to clump. More tips and tricks to using it (as well as alternative uses for this cleaner) can be found at www.queenoffree.net/2012/07/homemade-dishwasher-detergent-recipe.

6. I love using half.com, a subsidiary of eBay, to sell books. I typically price books just below the highest priced item. Save on packaging by reusing boxes and envelopes you receive, and be sure to send the books via media mail for the lowest postal rates.

Chapter 7: Formidable Foes and Fellow Debt Slayers

1. See, for example, "Good Debt vs. Bad Debt," *CNNMoney*, http://money.cnn .com/magazines/moneymag/money101/lesson9/index2.htm (accessed April 24, 2014).
2. "Friends and Family Influence Your Health Habits," *Huffington Post*, August 12, 2013, http://www.huffingtonpost.com/2013/08/12/friends-family-health-habits -smoking-drinking-alcohol_n_3728302.html. See also Nicholas A. Christakis and James H. Fowler, *Connected* (New York: Little, Brown and Company, 2009). This book examines how those in your social media networks also influence your choices. Find more information at http://www.connectedthebook.com.
3. From the "Friending" message series, LifeChurch.tv
4. To find a course near you, see http://daveramsey.com/fpu/classfinder or http://www.crown.org/AboutUs/FindCrown.aspx.
5. Mark 8:36, NIV

Chapter 8: Of Princes and Princesses

1. I'm sure it's theologically incorrect to imply that you and I make God cry. So perhaps it's better to point out that we might bring Him grief. I once witnessed someone telling her child that the reason it was raining was because God was sad. That made me wince. Hopefully, I didn't make you wince. It was a parallel metaphor and turn of phrase. Please don't send me hate mail.
2. Melanie Hicken, "Average Cost to Raise a Kid: $241,080," *CNNMoney*, August 14, 2013, http://money.cnn.com/2013/08/14/pf/cost-children (accessed April 24, 2014).
3. Matthew 7:9-11, NIV
4. Note to self: "Bread and Fish" and "Stones and Snakes" are both awesome potential band names.
5. See Deuteronomy 11:18-21.
6. Big love to Visit Indy and the Doing Indy community. You have brought us joy unspeakable.
7. If, by chance, you ever find yourself flying in a vintage trick plane in formation with two other airplanes over an enormous body of water, may I give you a few suggestions? (1) Don't come down with shingles the week you are scheduled for said flight. It will become incredibly uncomfortable when you begin to push into the seat, holding on for dear life. (2) Realize that hanging upside down is not nearly as unnerving as seeing another plane flying so close to you that you can wave at the other passenger and see him wave back and then begin to pick his teeth. (3) Take Dramamine. Better safe than sorry. I was glad I did even though

I don't typically have motion sickness. (4) Be sure that all of the dials in front of you are working, even if it doesn't matter. Seeing the fuel gauge point to "E" will elicit a baby panic attack, even when the pilot assures you his gauge reads "F." (5) If you decide to allow your seven-year-old daughter to watch from the ground so she can witness just how awesome her mom is, you might also want to bring another family member with you. Midflight, as you squeal in panic and delight, it might occur to you that a family friend who probably isn't best suited for the task may be now saddled with the responsibility of telling your sweet cherub that Mommy is swimming with the fishies at the bottom of Lake Michigan. (6) Relax, listen to the pilot's country playlist, and enjoy the ride, realizing that you will probably never have this opportunity again.

8. Stan and Jan Berenstain, *The Berenstain Bears and Too Much Birthday* (New York: Random House, 1986).

9. One of the Princess Youngest's best reactions at Christmas ever was over a box of Goldfish that we bought for her. She repeated, "Thank you" over and over again and gave us both hugs. It just goes to prove that a gift doesn't have to be dazzling to elicit a joyful and gracious response from a child.

10. "2013 Back to School: Spending Less, Shopping Smart," National Retail Federation, August 14, 2013, http://www.nrf.com/modules.php?name =Dashboard&id=53 (accessed April 24, 2014).

11. Andy Stanley, "Our Way, A Way," (sermon, North Point Community Church, Alpharetta, Georgia, September 9, 2012), http://futurefamily.org/#our-way-a-way.

12. See Jeremiah 29:11.

Chapter 9: Joy for the Journey: A Benediction

1. Mothers of Preschoolers; see http://www.mops.org.

2. Melody Carlson, *It's Not Funny, I've Lost My Money!* (Wheaton, IL: Crossway Books, 2000). Sadly, it appears the book is now out of print. If you ask nicely, I'll loan you my copy.

3. Don't know how to begin a relationship with God? Just like paying off debt, it's not complex. Take a simple moment to breathe a prayer acknowledging your need for God to lead your journey. Express your belief that Jesus came to earth with the divine mission of dying to give you true life. Rejoice in the fact that He did not remain in the grave but conquered death. Confess that your efforts fall short and realize your great need for God. Reach out to me or someone you know who has faith in God, and we'll help you find a community to grow your new faith. You won't regret this decision.

4. Actually, Brian went with us to the Texas Roadhouse, but he did not eat. He sat and watched, celebrating with us. He wanted to be intentional with his first real meal out.

5. Dave Ramsey invites his listeners to visit Financial Peace Plaza to watch him record his show and once they've paid off their debt, to scream "We're debt-free!" on air. For more information, see https://www.daveramsey.com/show/visit/.

To hear our debt-free call, go here: http://www.queenoffree.net/2012/04/on-being-on-dave-ramsey-show.

6. Blood:Water partners with grassroots organizations in Africa to address the HIV/AIDS and water crises. For more information, visit www.bloodwater.org.

7. My friend Dustin is an amazing musician. You should check him out. Since the songs are parodies, we don't have the coin to print them here. If you e-mail me, I might be able to respond with the lyrics. Find Dustin Stamper at https://www.facebook.com/pages/Dustin-Stamper/117304811615653.

A Note from Cherie

I INVITE YOU to visit www.slayingthedebtdragon.com, where you can share your own debt-slaying story and find free, useful printables to assist in your journey. When you turn the page, you'll find an example of one of these exciting printables—it's the perfect reminder and inspiration as you begin your debt-slaying journey.

I also encourage you to use hashtag #slaydebt to share encouragement with fellow debt slayers on Instagram, Twitter, and Facebook. We're better together, friends.

Help others know there is a way out. Spread the hope that is within you. Spark another's journey out of debt and remember why you've embarked on this path. Every time you save a dollar, pay off another sum, and practice contentment, you bring me great joy and encouragement. I can't wait to hear your story and see it unfold.

Name your own "dragon."

Use the space below to identify whatever foe is challenging you today. You can do it!
Go to **www.slayingthedebtdragon.com** for a free downloadable dragon printable and many more resources!

About the Author

SINCE 2008, CHERIE LOWE has been confidently wearing a plastic crown and encouraging others to dream big dreams. Together with her husband, Brian, Cherie paid off $127,482.30 in a little under four years. She scribed the ups and downs of their debt-slaying journey on her popular website, www.QueenOfFree.net.

A graduate of Asbury University, Cherie strongly believes that something can come from nothing and that there is always a way for her readers to simplify their lives and their budgets. More than anything, through speaking and the written word, Cherie longs for others to know that there is hope for getting their finances under control. Her family's story has appeared in the *Wall Street Journal*, Yahoo Finance, *Redbook* magazine, AOL Daily Finance, and more. Cherie and Brian reside in Greenwood, Indiana, along with their daughters, Anna and Zoe.

Join the court of the Queen of Free on Twitter (@thequeenoffree), on Facebook (www.facebook.com/thequeenoffree), or on Pinterest (www.pinterest.com/thequeenoffree) to find practical, money-saving tips and daily inspiration to slay the debt dragon.

Online Discussion *guide*

TAKE *your* TYNDALE READING
EXPERIENCE *to the* NEXT LEVEL

A FREE discussion guide for this book
is available at bookclubhub.net, perfect
for sparking conversations in your book
group or for digging deeper into the text
on your own.

www.bookclubhub.net

*You'll also find free discussion guides for
other Tyndale books, e-newsletters, e-mail
devotionals, virtual book tours, and more!*